SWITZERLAND TO ALASKA

JUST TO DIE

The true story of a Swiss Artist
determined to travel to the end of the earth
to challenge his spirit
and find his soul.

KRIS WILLIAMS

ISBN: 978-0-9995332-0-8   (Paperback Edition)

The author has recreated, in the nearest way possible, the events, locales
and conversations as told to her by Ruedi Glauser. In order to maintain
their anonymity in some instances, the author has changed the names of
some individuals to protect the privacy of these individuals. The names that
were not changed include Ruedi's teachers and professors at the Allgemeine
Gewerbeschule, his employer Joseph Müller-Brockmann, a trusty pilot named
Harold, and the Alaska Native, Mr. Henry, who generously welcomed Ruedi
into his village.

Book Design by Kris @ krisgraphics.com
Cover Design by Kris @ krisgraphics.com
Cover Photos by Ruedi Glauser*
Cover Fonts: *Dead Kansas* by Fabien Delage
Adobe Acumin Pro Condensed
Interior Chapter Head Font: *Dead Kansas*
Interior Body Font: *Cormorant Garamond*

*Ruedi Glauser is a pseudonym for the main character of this book.

Printed and bound in the USA
First Printing May, 2017

To contact the publisher visit:
www.kriswilliamsauthor.com

THIS IS RUEDI GLAUSER'S STORY AS TOLD TO ME...

And here is why I wrote it down:

Ruedi Glauser* is a multi-faceted artist whose sensitivity to the world around him opened my eyes to the wonder of it, and whose journey of self-discovery while wandering into the dark interior of Alaska created a template I used to ask important questions of myself.

If Ruedi could open my eyes and challenge my own personal growth, I thought, perhaps the story of his wilderness trek could help open eyes and encourage journeys of self-discovery in others, too.

So I wrote *Switzerland To Alaska: Just To Die* for those whose vision has been dimmed to the wonder of the world...and need someone to light a flame so they can see what they've been missing...

I wrote this book for those who have taken few journeys of self-discovery...and would appreciate a kind of paradigm to help them take one or two more...

I wrote *Switzerland To Alaska: Just To Die* for any adventurer who yearns to know where trekkers have gone before them, how those trekkers prepared, and the difference preparation makes in the outcome.

I wrote it for all people who crave adventure, urgently want to experience the thrill of a trip into the wild, but are content enough to take the journey through a writer's words.

I wrote it for the curious who wonder what growing up in Switzerland is like, what preparing for a sojourn alone in the wilderness of Alaska would require, and what transformation in the human psyche must occur to survive.

I wrote this book for *you* if you've been bold enough to think you've already been challenged to the fullest, and could benefit from a big dose of reality.

I wrote this book for *you* if you believe your circumstances in the life adventure you're undertaking at the moment are too difficult to overcome, and you need a big dose of inspiration.

If you are none of the above, but are one who simply desires to view the world more intently, then you are an artist and I wrote this book for you, too. Let it spark your creativity and fan your appreciation for all that lives.

*Ruedi Glauser is a pseudonym for the character whose true story this is.

DEDICATION

This book is dedicated to Ruedi Glauser*,
who believed I could tell his story,
and trusted me with his heart.

ACKNOWLEDGEMENTS

I give unending thanks to my husband, William, a detailed and long-suffering editor, and my daughter, Rachel, a thoughtful and encouraging reader. Without the aid and encouragement of either of these two, this book never would have been produced.

| 1 |

GLACIAL ENERGY

Each time I traverse a glacier, the explorer in me awakens, becoming acutely aware, carefully watching, remembering, comparing, and mentally noting the obvious as well as the subtle. My explorer ears capture sweet sounds or warning noises possibly helpful to my survival. In fact, all of my senses heighten to secure whatever information Mother Nature is capable of communicating. The explorer in me continually reassesses how best to move forward.

My father taught me how to approach a glacier. He did this not with words so much as by insisting that I observe and follow him. In the wintertime he would point out the glacier's crevices that had been covered by snow. "It's very dangerous to fall into one of those," he would say. "Always be aware, Ruedi. Always be aware of where the crevices lie."

Being aware meant being conscious of the pressure our feet exerted on the snow and responding to any changes. Our ears had to be awake to any alteration in the sound of our crunches. And we had to pay attention to how the glacier felt. We had to be open to the glacier's vibrations.

Perhaps you can understand what I am saying if I tell you that a glacier is very much like a human being. People constantly send out vibrations that can be detected, consciously or subconsciously. Vibrations are a person's energy. If in your presence a person is content or joyful, it is possible to feel his positive energy and you

may relax or become joyful yourself. If that same person thinks contrary thoughts, his vibrations will be modified, his mood will alter, and you will feel his anger or his sorrow without his even having to say a word. As it is possible to read the different moods of a person, to read his energy, my father was very good at reading the mood of a glacier and the mountains he walked upon. I sensed that he opened himself up and let all the surrounding vibrations flow into him.

My father never put it into words, but if he had, I think he would say that you must become a musical instrument and let the surroundings play you.

In my life I have come to see that everything is energy. Every surrounding presents its own electrical current that, if permitted, will play upon me a dirge, a rhapsody, a lullaby, an orchestral symphony, or a type of music I may never have heard. If I wish to move forward with confidence in a new landscape, I must become familiar with its vibrations, and allow them to pluck my strings.

It is possible to prevent outside vibrations from touching you. For most people, fear is a powerful human emotion that prevents incoming vibrations. But if you can release the fear, if you can let the vibrations in, then you will start to vibrate, and your vibrating will allow you to calmly proceed in harmony with all that surrounds you.

Before visiting Alaska, I never knew what fear was. I never recall being afraid of anything. Like my father, I vibrated with the mountains and glaciers around me.

I had met a lot of people who experienced fear, though. At one time or another I observed a person in a state of high anxiety, and could not understand why anyone would let himself become paralyzed by a force he didn't want to be controlled by.

For example, why were people afraid of heights when they still had a foothold on a piece of a mountain? Why were they afraid they would fall to their deaths if their body still had a touch point with the earth? That was a mystery to me.

Before Alaska, the fear of dying had never entered my mind.

In Alaska, that all changed.

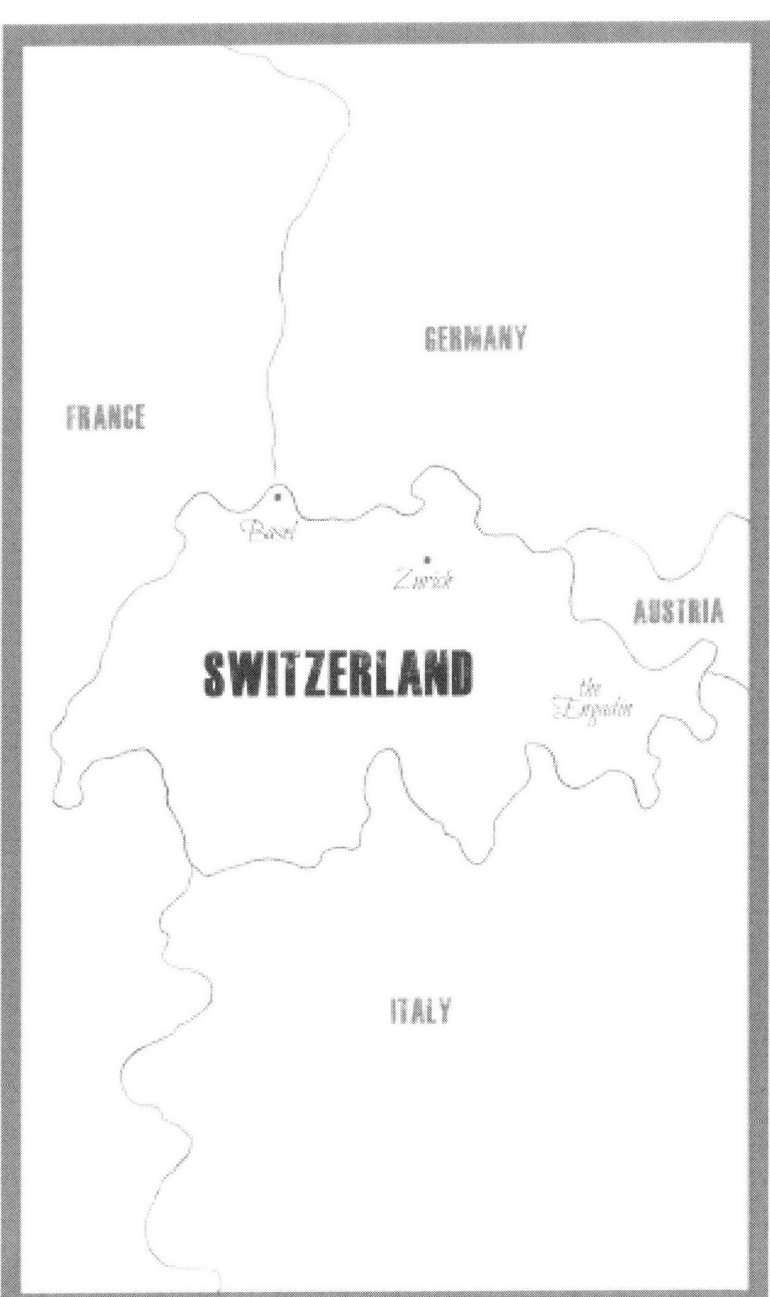

FRANCE

GERMANY

Basel

Zürich

AUSTRIA

SWITZERLAND

the
Engadin

ITALY

THE MARMOT

I was already an explorer by the time I was three years old, when the lower regions of the Swiss Alps pleaded for my attention. As soon as I could walk there probably wasn't a day that I didn't wander among the edelweiss, saunter around grassy knolls, skip through meadows, hike deserted trails, climb over boulders, shimmy through rock crevices, crawl along mountain walls, wade in mountain streams, or budge my way up and across hills and down valleys, looking out for whatever and whomever I might meet along the way. Rarely did I encounter another human being.

I did meet a marmot, though. During one of my springtime excursions he poked his gray snout out of a hole that bordered a small rock I had plopped down on for a rest. I said hello, and he showed me his large front teeth. When I showed him mine, he turned one small ear to me, and then the other.

"You needn't worry that I'll hurt you," I told him. "I'm just resting."

The marmot nodded his head and crawled all the way out of the hole, exposing a plump white belly and ginger-gray haunches. I told him I was a very long way from home, but that he shouldn't worry about that either. I would find my way back.

He wanted to know where my home was.

"Do you know where Samedan is?" I asked.

He stared at me, then shook his head.

"It's here in the Engadin!" I whispered, very surprised that he didn't know about my village.

The marmot looked embarrassed.

"Switzerland's a big place," I added in a tone that I hope comforted him. "I guess it's hard to know about every village in Switzerland."

The marmot and I became friends. I would always stop for a visit when I was traveling by. His snout would typically peep out of the hole as I drew close, and when I sang out a "Grüezi!" the marmot forced the rest of his fat, furry body into the sunshine. Usually the marmot crawled to a shelf of flat rock that overlooked the valley, and sat on his haunches gazing at me. Sometimes he looked away when I told him I had had a scary fall between two boulders. "That doesn't happen often," I assured him, "because Vati taught me how to use my feet." The marmot was always interested when I spoke about my father --- my Vati --- Hans Ruedi Glauser, and my life in Samedan.

Vati worked for the federal government as a Border Control Agent, and his job took him away from home often. Vati traveled from Samedan, my tiny village in Graubunden, the southeast part of Switzerland, toward the Italian border. He hiked along the Bernina Pass, where in the winter there are often avalanches and the weather is always very cold. Usually Vati built shelters along the way for himself to stay in --- sleep in even --- if the weather got too bad. He could be gone for weeks at a time, and my mother never knew exactly where he was.

My father was very withdrawn, spoke little, and was driven to repeat tasks until completing them perfectly. Although never diagnosed, people today would probably say that he was autistic. Yet he was a highly influential teacher over me. You don't always need words to teach. You can learn a lot from a person just by watching. In fact, that's probably the best way to learn how to ski.

But learning how to ski with Vati did have its drawbacks.

If I fell, Vati wouldn't say a word. He would only watch, wait, and while waiting say nothing until I got up. The truth is, his penetrating stares were almost always full of displeasure. There

would be no words, but I would feel him say, "Oh little Ruedi, you are not very smart. Don't you see? You did it again. Didn't I tell you already several times that you shouldn't pass me?" He would shake his head and I would sense his disappointment. "You are delaying our progress," his eyes would say.

He would never challenge me to compete with him, but I did anyway. And then I would fall, and the prize for my effort would always be a disapproving look.

After a while I stopped trying to pass my father on skis. It wasn't because I decided to be obedient. It was because I was discouraged in his presence. I only worked to get better when I wasn't with him. When I skied with my father it was more peaceful to watch and follow than to be criticized.

Nevertheless, watching my father was a treat. He was pure perfection on skis.

Vati was the only child of an alcoholic father and a very strict mother. My grandfather and grandmother divorced when my father was just a baby. After the divorce, my grandmother didn't allow her drunken husband to even visit.

Vati grew up in the Matte Quarter in Bern, close to the river Aare. The Matte Quarter was the poorest part of town in those days, and when there were floods, which happened every year, the streets all around his home were overrun by the river.

Vati always had to wear short pants, even in winter, and he owned only wooden shoes. He and his mother didn't have money for extravagances like long trousers and leather shoes. Yet there was enough money for food, because in his youth Vati weighed over one hundred kilos, or close to two hundred and twenty pounds. While trying to fill up the emotional emptiness in his life with food he became a large and pudgy boy and all the kids made fun of him.

But even so, he could ski. The poor people at that time took apart barrels --- old barrels that had once stored beer, for instance --- and used the planks as skis. It's very difficult to ski using those rounded boards, but my father did and was very good at it. He was also a good swimmer. But he stayed fat until his twenties, when he

decided to change his lifestyle. How did he lose weight? He was Swiss, and every Swiss boy who reaches the age of twenty must join the army. My father lost fifty pounds in the army and never found them again.

Once Vati took me to the Matte Quarter in Bern where he had grown up. He was proud to show me that he had succeeded, that he had pulled himself up out of poverty. He was very tender with me during those moments. But otherwise I was acutely aware that he never hugged me. And it was only at bedtime, after we prayed, that he would give me a good night kiss on the cheek.

My father taught me how to mountaineer on Piz Bernina, the highest mountain in the eastern Alps. Mountaineering is different from downhill skiing in that you use neither chairlifts nor groomed trails, nor do you use skis that have fixed-heel bindings. Instead, you use cross-country-type skis to climb whatever mountain you choose, on your own power. The bottoms of the skis have to be prepared with seal skins, using a special glue to attach the skins to the ski base. The seal skins hold fur that grows stiffly in one direction and, when rubbed the opposite way, will stick or hold to the snow. You can get a picture of what seal skin does when you rub the hair on the back of a dog. If you rub the hair one way, the hair lies flat. If you rub it in the opposite direction, the hair will stand up. Seal skin fur is short and thick and can be applied to the bottom of skis so that when the skis are used on an incline, the seal hair will not lie flat but will rise up and grab the snow. With mountaineering skis Vati and I would be able to climb without sliding backwards. When we reached the top of our mountain, we would take off the seal skins, sand the glue, and ski back down.

One afternoon we mountaineered on the slope above the Morteratsch Glacier, and skied all the way to the boulders at the glacier's mouth. That day Vati asked me repeatedly to ski in his tracks. He warned me that I shouldn't go away from his tracks because ditches and cracks abounded and he didn't want me to fall into any of them. He taught me to recognize where the crevices lie by pointing out that the snow that covered the crevices was always slightly darker.

I went behind him, watching where he went, always following.

As my father gracefully moved across the fresh-fallen snow, he explained how the glacier underneath him had formed.

"Glaciers grow from one layer of snow that remains in one area all year round," he said. "Every new season of fresh-fallen snow adds another layer, and each additional layer adds more weight to the snow beneath it. Everything below the new snow gets compacted."

He dug about two feet into our ski run with his pole and jabbed the pole into the ground.

"Hear that?" he asked. "It's not hard ice. It's ice that's still forming. My pole is poking through it a little bit. But with more time the ice will get more tightly compressed. Then it'll be so thick I won't be able to stick my pole into it at all. Maybe that'll take twenty years, or maybe it'll take a hundred. Eventually, though, dense ice recrystallizes into those fine grains that you see at the bottom of the glacier's edge."

I learned that a glacier forms at a higher, colder part of a mountain, from where it cuts a sliding path down into the valley. Glaciers are always growing or contracting, and gravity pulls them downward. What makes movement possible is a fine water film between the glacier and the rock it sits on. From the movement and the water underneath the ice, various cracking, hissing and popping noises escape. There's quite a range of noises on a glacier, especially in summer, because of melting ice and glacial movement. But a glacier doesn't just melt in summer. Even in milder winters a glacier can melt away. Vati explained all these things to me, using more words than normal when we were outside on our own.

He would say, "If you ski off-slope, you have to always be aware of the possibility of avalanches." He would tell me to "Look up! Be aware of how sharply the mountain slants above us. Can you see if there's a buildup of new snow?" I learned to be especially aware of snow buildup after a period of intense snowfall. The steeper the slope of the mountain above us, the greater would be the chance of an avalanche. It's easy for a snowdrift to break off from its home when it becomes too heavy for its position. Even a loud noise could invite a breakaway. "You can never say, 'It's safe now,'" my father warned.

When we weren't skiing on the glacier my father and I would ski on Piz Diavolezza, Piz Lagalb, Piz Corvatsch, Piz Nair and Trais Fluors, all mountains in the Bernina Range of the Alps near St. Moritz.

But I never forgot my first T-Bar lift in Samedan. From there I got to know the woods around our home, and the creatures that abounded in them. In wintertime Vati pointed out to me animal tracks that are impossible to see in summertime. He showed me the differences among the hooves of the chamois, the ibex, and the red deer. We saw pine marten tracks that would lead right to a tree and disappear. Tracks can tell you stories about what animals pass along the way, as well as let you know which are male and which are female. Vati knew which tracks to follow to find a sheltering cave, and which ones to avoid. He never told me that he killed animals to eat while he was working, but I bet he did. I knew he carried a gun. My father helped me imagine who lived in the woods so close to our home, and who passed by. Once we filled a deer print with plaster of Paris, so that I could take it home with me to see what it looked like.

Besides being an expert skier, mountain climber, and animal tracker, my father was also skilled in crafts, drawing and calligraphy. He made a xylophone that sounded out beautifully clear notes when someone struck its panels with a mallet. He made a very functional wooden puppet that a person could operate with long strings and slats.

I always sat beside Vati in the evenings, watching carefully as he worked on his wood carvings. Only after many, many hours of doing this did he allow me to touch his tools, and after many more hours passed did he allow me to use one of them. I commenced my first artistic endeavor by hacking off thick chunks from a stump of wood that I had selected and pinned between my knees. Vati glanced over at me from time to time, but would not say anything to guide me. When I cut myself, however, he complained, "You should have used the knife more carefully." I could never shake the feeling of stupidity whenever Vati criticized me.

One winter day I decided to "create" a wooden bowl. I selected a fat piece of pinewood and immediately began digging into its

center --- the part that would hold the soup or cereal. As a boy of six, how could I properly judge how thick the wood was? How could I know my little knife would pierce the bottom? How could I know that my knife would take out a piece of the kitchen table as well?

"Anyone would know that you don't force a knife so deeply through a piece of wood like that," my father insisted. After that I put down the knife, and did not pick it up again for a long, long time. I became content just watching my father work. It was more peaceful that way.

I remember that Vati had a nice organization to his tools. He drew and wrote calligraphy with goose feather quills, which he kept in a drawer in the kitchen. He carried his wood carving tools in a wooden box that he kept in his bedroom. Mother mostly knitted beside him when he worked.

She was a good cook, my mother. My father, not at all. Cooking was one thing he could not do. Once he had to prepare lunch because my mother was visiting a friend in town. My father filled a pot with water, took a can of ravioli from the cupboard, and put the unopened can in the pot of water until the water boiled. He heated our lunch in this way, explaining that it was the best way to cook ravioli. Even at six years old, I was skeptical.

"What about your mother?" the marmot asked. "Where is your Mueti when you're out here all alone?"

"She's with my big sister, Kathrin," I patiently explained to him. "Kathrin takes care of Mueti when Vati and I are taking care of the mountains."

I told the marmot about our apartment in Samedan. It was part of a 4-story house that was huddled next to a barn. The proprietors of the building were two ladies who lived on the first floor. They worked the property as a small farm. In the building we had central heating, and therefore no need of a fireplace in the middle of our living room, which many of the other houses in the Engadin had and used regularly. Nevertheless, from the forest my sister and I did need to collect firewood every week. My mother burned it in the basement of the building to heat a huge pan of water in order to wash our clothes. After the clothes were clean,

she hung them out to dry on our balcony. A couple of hours after having been hung outside, Kathrin and I dragged the stiff (and in winter) frozen pieces of underwear, sweaters, shirts, socks, and sheets from the line. The mountain air was so dry that, even in winter, the clothes were all ready to fold and put away.

It was a typical Engadin home with thick walls and Romansch drawings carved into the clay exterior around the doors and windows. The building's windows were a bit larger than our neighbors', and our apartment's living room bay window looked out over all the mountains that surrounded Samedan. Still, I thought the house was gray and ugly and remember almost nothing from inside our apartment. No colors, patterns, sounds, nor smells.

I didn't feel at home there, so spent most of my time outside, hours on end. Every morning in the winter I'd yank on my wool socks and leather shoes, wool sweater, jacket and mittens, pull down a wool cap as far as I could over my thick head of hair, and skedaddle out for a day in the snow. I took nothing else with me except my curiosity about how the world looked. I had no earmuffs. My wool cap would ride up and my ears would look out. Sometimes they got so cold I could feel nothing in them. I remember my fingers becoming so cold that when I took off my mittens, the snow felt warm to the touch. After spending just a few minutes back inside the apartment, the ache that came with defrosting my fingers was like the sharp stabbing of a million needles. Yet I went out to wander around, by myself, again and again.

I wandered by myself, that is, until Reguli moved into the apartment above us.

| 3 |

REGULI & LEAVING SAMEDAN

Her given name was Regula, but her mother called her Reguli, and so did I. She wore her white blond hair in two braids, had freckles, and smiled at me whenever I looked at her. She was soft and pretty like a flower. I loved her. She was five years old and I was four.

There is a feast in the Engadin called *Chalandamarz*, which celebrates the coming of spring. With artificial flowers, large cowbells and a parade, the children of the Engadin "push out" the winter. It begins on the first day of March, when each young boy dresses in a herdsman costume and wraps a wide leather belt around his waist. He then hangs on his belt a cowbell as large as his belt can hold.

A boy himself usually doesn't make the artificial flowers that he attaches to his woolen cap or belt as part of the Chalandamarz costume. Instead, he asks a girl he knows to make the flowers for him. As a "thank you," the boy invites the girl to the evening dance. But after dressing and before the dance all of the children march about as the boys clang their bells with enough melody and noise to "chase away" winter. The parade pauses in front of houses in town, and the children serenade the home dwellers with simple spring songs that ask the grass to grow and the snow to go. If there are people in the houses listening to the serenade, they give out apples, cookies, small cakes, or even money to the minstrels. Then everybody brings the treats together for an evening feast, which is

followed by games and the dance.

The spring right before I turned five, I asked Reguli to make the Chalandamarz flowers for me. She did, and that night I sat with her at the dance, although she did not dance with me. It was not because she was too shy. It was because neither of us knew how.

In the summer of that year, Reguli asked me, "What makes a boy a boy?"

I didn't know how to answer. I shrugged. "What makes a girl a girl?" I asked back.

The corners of her soft lips turned up, and she said, "I know a place where we can go to find out."

So I followed her along a path that took us in the direction of a lumberyard at the edge of town. We slipped into the warehouse where beautiful, freshly milled arve wood, a type of Swiss pine, was stacked high around us. Engadin houses can retain the arve's fresh scent for years.

Reguli sniffed, and smiled. She looked at me, and I at her. A shaft of golden light filtered down from one of the windows high above us and the storeroom was very peaceful. Reguli removed her shoes, I removed mine. She took off her jumper, I took off my shirt. She unbuttoned her blouse, I unbuttoned my trousers. She took off her underwear, I took off mine. Soon we stood there naked. We looked and touched. They weren't sexual looks and touches. They were looks and touches motivated by curiosity. What makes a girl a girl? How is she different from me? I still remember the smell of Reguli's skin. It was fresh, like strawberries and cream.

A woodworker from the shop came in and saw our clothes strewn about and our bodies completely naked. He ran straight to Reguli's mother and told her. By the time she came running to us, angry and shouting, we were dressed again. I didn't feel we had done anything wrong. I didn't understand why she was so angry.

I think we were curious one more time after that. But then the curiosity passed.

Reguli joined Kathrin and me one day the following winter when we went sledding. We chose Piz Nair as our mountain for the day. It was a good hour's walk from home.

We had one sled and with it climbed up and slid down the mountain fifty times or more, until the light began to fade and snow began to fall. Faster and faster the snow came so we gathered our sled and each other's hands to head toward home. The blizzard snow stung our cheeks and poured into our mouths when we tried to speak. We couldn't see the trail toward our house nor could we see the mountains in the distance. I couldn't even see my hand in front of my face. Kathrin started to cry. Reguli sat down on the sled and didn't move. I bent down and leaned into her face. There was fear in her eyes.

That fear produced a conviction in my belly which made me straighten up, turn my head in the direction I knew we needed to go, and calmly begin pulling the sled behind me. Kathrin followed. She took the rope of the sled when I struggled on an uphill slope. Her crying turned to intermittent sobs. I think my silent march comforted her somehow. And Reguli never said a word.

When we reached our house, we crept up the stairs and found my mother and Reguli's mother waiting on the stairwell hugging each other. When it sunk in that all three of us were standing right there on the apartment steps, tears of relief washed over them.

In the spring of my seventh year Vati began an advanced education course with the federal government in order to be qualified for a "better" job. As a result, in the autumn of that year he was promoted and would no longer have to trek through the mountains in winter's snow and ice when conditions were treacherous. Instead, he would sit at a desk. His new job would be to track down the "big fish" who worked for groups or companies which transported goods across the border illegally. Vati would get to play detective from the security of an office. Vati's new job meant that he, Mueti, Kathrin and I would have to move away from Samedan and the mountains I loved, to Kreuzlingen, a small lakeside town in northeast Switzerland.

I watched everyone pack, but I could not help. I kept wanting everyone to put everything back in its place in our apartment, where it belonged.

So instead of helping I went out to say goodbye to my marmot. On that day I met a hunter who showed me his fresh game.

Hunters shoot marmots in autumn. I knew that. I expected that. They like to rub the oil from the marmot fat onto their arthritic joints with the hope that the marmot oil will make the pain go away. What I did not expect to see was a hunter carrying a marmot with a telltale splash of reddish fur across its back and between its eyes. The hunter had shot my friend.

When my family and I reached the train station in Samedan with all of our personal belongings, Reguli and her parents were there to see us off. Reguli handed me a red paper flower.

"This is to use if you come back for the Chalandamarz," she said.

From the window I saw her wave goodbye, but she was not smiling.

Nor was I. My return wave was a heartsick wave not simply because I was leaving Reguli. My return wave was heartsick because I was also leaving the place where I had lived and breathed and felt most alive. On the train my soul screamed out in agony, but I made no sound. My heart was aching, but I did not cry. I felt as if I were being torn out of the ground by the roots. All of my senses had been heightened in the Engadin.

In Kreuzlingen, they would close down, one by one.

| 4 |

ALMIGHTY DEATH

Maybe it was because my senses had shut down that I came to believe I could never die. Even when death stared me right in the face, I still believed it couldn't touch me.

From the time I was seven years old until I was twelve, my family traveled back up to the Engadin during the holidays. We would do mountaineering in the winter and hiking in the summer. So for a brief time each year my senses would be teased, and my invincibility tested.

The summer after I turned twelve my father bought a car and we --- my mother, father, sister and I --- planned a trip to a mountain valley right before the Engadin. It was the first car Vati could afford, and he was very proud of it.

We left Kreuzlingen on the first Saturday in July. Although snow still frosted the mountains that day, we did not plan to ski. So in my father's car we packed only hiking boots, clothing and gloves that would protect us against rain and cold, and some food supplies. From Kreuzlingen we drove to a mountain hut close to Preda, about 6,000 feet above sea level. The hut belonged to a friend of my father. There was no plumbing, no electricity, and for cooking and washing we had to carry water from the well outside. The kitchen and living room were on the bottom floor of the hut. The living room walls were flat wood planks --- in fact the whole house was made of wood except for the roof, which was made of tin. Anyone could always hear even the sound of a gentle rain on

the roof, yet I could sleep right through the loudest storm.

The hut had no fireplace, but it did have a stove for cooking. The stove was fixed in place between dark wood cabinets nailed to the wall and two other cabinets that stood on the floor. The main room, the living room, had a table and chairs, candles, and a tablecloth. We climbed a wooden ladder to reach two small bedrooms located above the living room and kitchen. Inside the rooms were only beds, pillows, covers, sheets and pillowcases.

The hut was unheated, unlit, and undecorated. It was simple. Barren. Yet it was all heaven to me and I loved it. We didn't plan on spending time inside the hut anyway unless it rained or snowed.

On the 6th of July it did snow, but by the 10th, the snow around our hut was gone. It was then that Uncle Hugo and Tanta Emma brought my cousin Cedric for a visit. Cedric was two years older than I, a good hiker, and every time we saw each other we renewed our easy friendship. My aunt and uncle had planned to stay the day and everybody did a hike together toward the east, to the summit of the Albula Pass. We knew nearby there was a small restaurant where for lunch we could enjoy hot soup and tea. After the hike my aunt and uncle left and Cedric stayed behind to finish the vacation with us.

Two days later Vati said that he wanted Kathrin, Cedric and me to join him on a hike. This time Vati decided we would go north, toward Piz Muot.

We figured it would take about four hours to reach the summit, where Vati said we would eat the lunch we had packed: sandwiches of bread and cheese, peeled and cut carrots, apples, water, hot tea and strawberry fruit-flavored syrup that my mother often used to make drinks for us children and which I always hated. All of us dressed in long-sleeved shirts, hiking pants that finished just below the knee, socks, hiking boots and woolen caps. We carried neither gloves nor sunglasses, but Vati, as usual, pocketed his pipe. Smoking a pipe was his way of laying off smoking too many cigarettes. He didn't smoke his pipe while walking, only when resting.

We hiked a couple of hours on trails at the beginning, but later climbed around rocks and boulders and up steep mountain walls.

Being without ropes made what we were doing quite difficult, and also quite dangerous. We could easily have fallen. Kathrin decided to stay further down, and did not seek the summit. The three of us men continued to the top where we had a short rest. We sat there on our own rock peaks, looking out over the mountains around us. Then we started down.

I suggested using the opposite side of the mountain from which we had climbed up. We had already proven ourselves by conquering the rocky cliffs, and scaling down the same way we came up would be too much for one day. On the other side of the mountain I noticed a snow-filled ravine. We could walk down that way. Or did we need to walk? Why not a more interesting and rewarding method? Maybe we could slide!

Where Kathrin stayed down below in the grass she had a beautiful view all around. We didn't worry that she couldn't see us as we descended.

The patch of snow started just a little bit below the crest of the mountain. All three of us tested the crusty powder by sliding in our boots, pretending we were skiing. We were still right at the top but it was quickly becoming a competition.

We were all laughing. "Who's the fastest?" Vati yelled. Maybe it was because my father wanted to show off in Cedric's presence that he offered such a challenge. Or maybe it was because Vati was feeling strong enough to beat me in boots. Vati hadn't challenged me on skis on any mountain since I was six years old. I think he was afraid I had become too skilled for him to beat me. Had I beaten him, I think his spirit would have suffered. I don't think he would have known what to do. When I skied with my father, he insisted I stay in his tracks. If I happened to go around him because I wanted to get better, I almost always managed to fall. But between the time I was six and now at twelve, I had practiced a lot on my own. When we lived in Samedan and Vati was working I skied every day there was snow. When we moved to Kreuzlingen, I skied on school trips, in ski camps and with friends. I had gotten much better. And Vati knew it.

On this day, however, we were wearing boots, not skis. And on this day, Cedric, possessing an impressionable young mind,

accompanied us. Whatever the reason, I was immediately caught up in the excitement of the race. I got caught up in the exhileration of the challenge. Maybe I was wrong in thinking Vati's spirit would suffer if I beat him. Maybe I needed to show my father that I was strong and skilled. Maybe I'd win his approval by beating him! I believed I could beat him. To beat him I knew I simply had to open up my senses to vibrate with the mountain.

Vati started down the ravine first, and I followed, soon leaving Cedric quite a way behind me. Then Vati gained in speed. I worked to pass him. I felt strong and moved surely. I was just getting ahead when one of Vati's legs broke through the snow. It was as if a stationary trap had reached up and grabbed onto the bottom half of Vati's right leg. My father fell flat on his chest. Hard. He just lay there. Stopped in his tracks. I laughed because my FATHER had fallen down and if anyone was going to fall I would have been the one! I climbed back up the few feet that I had passed him, still giggling. Then I saw that he was hurt. He was lying there and couldn't breathe. Now I was very embarrassed. Cedric had not laughed.

Cedric finally reached us and looked at me with scared eyes. I didn't say anything.

Finally my father got up, and we slowly finished our way to the meadow where Kathrin waited. We all sat down on the grass and had our sandwiches and tea for lunch. No one said anything. It was an uncomfortable silence. There was a low vibration in the air that stirred my stomach. After we finished eating, my father didn't smoke his pipe, something he normally would have done after a meal.

While we were gathering up the remains of lunch, Vati said, "I don't feel well. I will not be able to continue." Those words struck me like lightning. My father never gave up. He finished everything.

"I'm going to sit here while you go and get help." He said it as a suggestion, not a command. He looked off into the distance.

So Kathrin stayed, and Cedric and I went.

In this one instance I should tell you that I was afraid. But the fear wasn't for me at all. It was for my father.

Cedric and I ran back down Piz Muot the way we had come.

On a rocky slope I fell, cutting skin away from my arm. I picked myself up without thought and again ran so fast that I reached the limit of my strength. Even Cedric, fourteen years old to my twelve, couldn't keep up with my adrenaline-fed body. We ran to the mountain hut, and I couldn't get the words out fast enough for my mother. "Vati is hurt! He fell! I don't know exactly what happened! He needs help! Can you get someone right away?"

Before this day none of the neighboring huts had had any occupants. But on this day, my mother told me, the neighbors had arrived. What luck! We had no phone and mother couldn't drive the car. One of the neighbors kindly offered to drive Mueti to a Preda hotel where there would be a public telephone. The other neighbor went to where I told him my father waited. He knew the mountains well and understood exactly where I explained my father was resting. Cedric and I stayed at the hut. I don't remember what I did.

I do remember that Mueti came back up and told us she had called the airport in Samedan. She had old friends there from the time Vati worked in Samedan as a border control agent. She told her friends that they should come with a helicopter to rescue my father. They promised to do what needed to be done, and Mother returned to the hut where Cedric and I waited.

After three hours, we were still waiting. Mother went down to the hotel again, and found out that a rescue team was arriving by train. They were going to go up to my father on foot!

"I asked for a helicopter!" Mueti cried out in dismay.

"Rescue via helicopter costs a lot of money!" one of the team members said. "Dr. Schmidt ordered this plan of operation."

Mueti insisted that there was not enough time. That already too much time had been wasted. She called again to the Samedan airfield. She explained again what had happened to my father all the while Dr. Schmidt screamed in her ear that she was being insubordinate.

A helicopter arrived in Preda within fifteen minutes and an agitated Dr. Schmidt entered the bubbled flying machine. The pilot and the doctor took off immediately for the meadow at Piz Muot.

We found out later that Dr. Schmidt was afraid of flying, and had regularly failed to request a helicopter rescue when immediate response was surely called for. In fact, we later learned, he had never passed his medical board certification. Upon arriving at the rescue site, he examined my father. After determining that my father was having difficulty breathing, he injected him with some sort of substance, presumably to allow greater ease for his lungs to expand and contract. Because the helicopter was only a two-seater, my father, the patient, had to be strapped to a stretcher and tied to the landing skids in order to be transported to the hospital. The helicopter lifted into the air while Kathrin and our neighbor watched. It was a seven-minute ride to the hospital from the meadow where they had waited. During those seven minutes, my father died.

The hospital could do nothing to revive him.

Kathrin was fifteen years old when my father died. She had waited by him for hours that seemed like days, all the while not knowing what was going on inside of him, not knowing what he was suffering. Kathrin still is not able to talk about her experience there. She is very like my father was, I think. Her handwriting is very similar to his. Mine not at all.

Kathrin did tell us later that a German woman with her son had passed by and lingered for a while, helping to watch over my dad. The woman and her son took photos that day and later sent them to my mother. When the woman found out that my father died that day, she said she wouldn't have sent the photos if she had known.

When the helicopter left to gather up Vati, the neighbor who had been driving my mother from place to place drove my mother over the Albula Pass to the hospital in Samedan.

While my mother was gone this second time, I waited impatiently in the hut, then went to find solace in the outhouse. Enclosed in such a space I could concentrate on praying to God that my father wouldn't die, even though I knew already that he had. So my prayers became that God would do for Vati what He had done for Lazarus --- restore him back to life.

The day before the hike I had been given signs, warnings against

going up that mountain the following day. The signs came with a feeling of foreboding, and the feeling was even stronger in the morning on the day of the hike.

What happens is that I see pictures, really clear pictures. On the day before that hike I saw a picture of Piz Muot falling apart. I was embarrassed to tell anybody about it.

I had seen other pictures before, by the way, and had always been afraid of them. They disturbed me because I didn't know what they meant. The pictures were always in color, clear and detailed. For one warning there would usually be more than one picture, but they did not come together as a video. They were only still frames.

I never saw myself in those pictures. I almost never saw any people at all. I saw still frames showing an event that had just happened. The pictures were of thunderstorms, rain, or rock avalanches --- things that in my world would make me think of having to be careful when I'm outside. They didn't come at a particular time of day or season, they just came.

I understand now that the pictures were warnings of a situation or a person that I was to watch out for or stay away from.

I was afraid to tell Vati --- afraid that he'd laugh. And with my father, once he had announced his plan, it was not to be questioned. You couldn't say, "I'd prefer to do something else today instead of going on that hike." In fact, Vati would often announce to my mother, "This weekend we do a hike." He wouldn't discuss the idea with her. He alone would make the decision.

No ideas about how to thwart the Piz Muot hike occurred to me until we had started on our way. After walking just a few hundred yards, I finally blurted out, "My hat, I need my wool hat with the tassel!"

I was hoping my father would get frustrated and say that our little expedition didn't have time for me to go back and get my hat if we wanted to complete the hike in one day. I wanted him to say that if I really needed to go back, then we would just have to cancel the whole trip. I was hoping that he would tell us that.

I wasn't even going to mind his frustration.

I was hoping he was going to say, "We'll all just have to turn around and go back."

And he would look at me and blame me. But that day I didn't care if he blamed me.

I was willing to be blamed, if he would just call off the hike.

But that didn't happen.

| 5 |

STICKS & ROLLING STONES

After the death of my father, the warning pictures stopped coming to me. Or if they came, I refused to look at them. In any case, when my mind goes back to those first few years in Kreuzlingen, all I see from that time is undeveloped film. Everything is blank.

Memories are stored in the file folder labeled "Teen Years," though. Mostly because of time spent with two sets of cousins. One set were the children of my mother's twin brother that included Cedric, the cousin who was with me when my father died, and his sister, Helene, four years my senior. Cedric and Helene visited us in the mountains during summer vacations, or for short ski holidays in winter.

The other set of cousins included Henrik and Walter, children of my mother's older brother and frequent companions during the time my family lived in Kreuzlingen. Henrik's and Walter's parents, my aunt and uncle, owned a landscaping company near Zurich, and in my middle school years, I spent my holidays working there. Henrik and Walter liked showing and sharing with their younger cousin all the stuff their parents bought for them. For instance, my cousins were proud motorcycle owners and insisted "little Ruedi" test out each one. Mueti had forbidden me to ride, but I disobeyed. My mother just didn't understand that I was invincible. I had never actually confided in her that death could not reach me because I didn't know exactly how to explain

it. How does a thirteen-year-old tell an adult that he is in control? So I rode my cousins' motorcycles.

Henrik also had a great collection of rock music that he was willing to share, and he introduced me to the Rolling Stones, a band that at that time was labeled as a radical alternative to the Beatles. That label interested me, and their music and image captured me. I could be a radical, too. For my parents my outward demeanor remained obedient and proper, but on the inside I would rise up and revolt, just like the Rolling Stones. The sad part was that at the time I didn't understand English.

To fill in our free time, Henrik, Walter and I played hide-'n'-seek games in the local Swiss sewer systems. To protect ourselves, we always carried with us sticks and candles. These proved quite handy for our survival. The sticks were for fighting off rats --- nice animals, actually, because they left us alone when they saw we were men with sticks --- and the lit candles were used as warning signals: if the wicks went out, that was a sign that there was something other than oxygen flowing through the pipes and we should escape from the sewer before being overcome by a poisonous gas.

At the end of ninth grade, one of my teachers suggested I take an exam for the next year's *VorKurs*, a one-year study program meant to equip me for further education. *VorKurs* in German means *Course Before*, and the VorKurs was a preparatory program for the *Fachschule*, a three-year course of study similar to an American technical or vocational school for the applied arts. The test was a five-day event that included drawing, German literature, math, history, science, and a secondary language, which for me was French.

You should know that I didn't choose this path for myself. It was imposed upon me by my teacher, with my mother's behind-the-scenes prodding. I never saw myself as an artist. My father was the artist, not I. I had simply watched him do his work.

But my test scores were good, and I was accepted into a VorKurs in St. Gallen.

St. Gallen is an hour's train ride from Kreuzlingen. If I wanted to be at school on time, I had to take the 5:30 AM train, which meant

that on the morning of every school day, I had to be up at five. But being up at five didn't mean that I had time for breakfast. That was the radical in me: I would show them! *I won't eat breakfast!* I never did, and still had to run to catch the train. But I never missed it. That was the me that was disciplined, obedient, mistake-free.

After the VorKurs and before entering the Fachschule, I was required to choose my field of study. Did I want to become a photographer, a designer, a painter or a sculptor? I said I wanted to be a Graphic Designer, even though I wasn't sure what Graphic Designers did. I had seen some nice graphics posters around town, and I liked what I saw. So I met with a test administrator to find out what I had to do to prepare for the Fachschule entrance exam.

"Only the best artists become designers, you know," the administrator said. He reminded me of my father and my shoulders slumped.

"And anyway, designers don't make much money," he added after seeing my shoulders. I went home thinking I would not even try to take the test. I was not confident in my artistic skills, even after the VorKurs. At that moment I didn't know what I wanted to do with my life. I went home to listen to my new Rolling Stones album.

My mother came out of the little turtle shell she had sunk into since the death of my father and marched herself downtown to sign me up for the Fachschule entrance exam. So because I was signed up, and because my mother had taken away my Rolling Stones album, and my stereo, I pulled myself out of my radical shell and sat for the exam.

When I learned that I had passed, I found out there was no Fachschule in Kreuzlingen. I would have to go back to St. Gallen! But with the Fachschule's extended school hours, I knew it would be unwise to once again spend over two-and-a-half hours of a school day on a train. And I couldn't arrange to stay in St. Gallen, either. After the death of my father, my family did not have sufficient money to send my sister or me away to school. I did receive a scholarship from the federal government for the Fachschule, but it wasn't enough to cover room and board as well as tuition.

So I looked across the lake to Konstanz, a small town in Germany, where there was a school that taught Graphic Design. The problem for me was that it was a Fachhochschule, a higher-level program that was really for graduates of the Fachschule. I decided to approach the administrators in my explorer mode, and they allowed me to show my grades and my work. After a short consideration they admitted me, a 16-year-old, into their university.

For four years I took the ferry from Kreuzlingen to Konstanz, where I attended art classes at the Fachhochschule Konstanz. Going to school in Germany was less expensive than going to school in St. Gallen, and I got what others would say was a very acceptable education. But after all was said and done, I felt that something in my life was missing. I felt it, but couldn't say what it was.

I don't know whether the sentiment had to do with anything spiritual, but I can tell you that I had stopped believing in God. He hadn't answered my prayers regarding my father. My father's life was the most important request I had ever made of God. Because God did not come through for me, I convinced myself that he wasn't worth believing in. He wasn't to be counted on. He had let me down.

I guess my spirit retracted into its own little turtle shell that shut itself tightly away.

What I was experiencing at the end of the Fachhochschule that I could explain was a feeling of ambivalence. I was two people who could not be joined. As an artist, turmoil reigned. Even though outwardly I gave the impression that I was confident and skilled, inside I felt untrained, unskilled, and unsure. As an explorer, though, I was perfect. I felt sure, aware, and tuned in. In the mountains I never feared any challenge or trial, and in fact went out of my way to seek them. Then I began to seek them even in the jobs I worked during school vacations.

One summer I worked the nightshift at an aluminum factory. My job was to gather up the factory's waste foil, aluminum cut-offs that had not been used in the factory's processing or could not be used in the manufacturing of its clients' products. Every day

this waste foil was blown into big cast-off rooms. I was required to press the foil together for reuse. The rooms were very hot and humid, the air acrid, and the work hard. I drank five or six quarts of water every night.

Two other vacation jobs involved preparing films for printing in a printing shop, and interning in an advertising agency doing layouts and logos.

The last summer job during my Fachhochschule years was the one I enjoyed most of all. For it I was relocated to a cheese hut in the mountains, taking care of farmers' cows and producing cheese for them. I spent six delicious weeks of waking up to the soft tinkling of bells, the fresh smell of peat moss and pine, breathing in the cool mountain air, and drifting off to sleep along with the mournful notes of the goatherds' nightly prayers being sung across the mountains. My thumbs got so big from milking the cows twice a day that I thought I would not be able to hold a drawing pencil again. Nevertheless I wanted to stay. But of course I couldn't. Even cows have to come down from the mountaintops eventually.

After finishing the Fachhochschule, I decided to go to Ireland, alone, for six months. Time was on my side. For six months I had all that money saved up from my summer work and nothing else to do. Sadly, the Rolling Stones hadn't helped me learn English. When I stepped off the plane onto Ireland's shore, I could say "yes," "no," and not much else. But after six months, I ended up with a proficiency in English that I carry with me to this day.

During all of my years of education from middle school on, I received no warning pictures of impending danger. No signs came to alert me. During that whole time they left me alone. Or I refused to let them in.

Even when I was issued a gun.

| 6 |

THE SWISS GRID

If two sets of equidistant parallel lines intersect at right angles, they will form a square. If more intersecting parallel lines are added to the square, they will, when taken together, form a grid. This grid can be superimposed on maps, charts, and other similar representations of the Earth's surface in an accurate and consistent manner in order to permit identification of ground locations, and plot distances from one set of locations to another.

A grid can also be employed to help define or organize information, systems or people.

Every Swiss boy, after birth, is placed on a grid.

From the time he is born his life is plotted out by the government. One of those plots on the grid requires that after eighteen and before the age of twenty, each Swiss male must join the Army.

The army's Basic Training Course, or *Rekrutenschule*, brings together from all over the country one hundred guys to a designated campsite for eighteen weeks. When I returned from Ireland, it was my appointed time to join the Army. The location of my basic course, however, was different from a regular Rekrutenschule campsite.

After the Second World War there was a regulation in Switzerland that required every newly constructed home to

include an underground bomb shelter that was supposed to be stocked with food and equipment that would last for two weeks in case of a nuclear attack. There were many such shelters built, and even large offices and warehouses had them. During my basic training --- from July to November --- all of the outdoor campsites were full with other recruits. So the government put my unit in one of those atomic cellars. From the time of its construction until that summer of my twentieth year, the cellar had remained pressurized so that no gasses or fumes would have been able to enter the living area had there been a nuclear attack. So when my unit and I spent our weeks of basic training down there in that tightly enclosed space, we all felt more than one kind of pressure. The basement rooms were also smelly; the latrines were under the ground with us, and there we were, one hundred guys, many of whom had had no personal hygiene education, sleeping next to one another in bunk beds.

The thicker the lines of the grid, the more like bars they become, and the thicker the bars, the more like a prison they feel.

One purpose of the Swiss grid is to require soldiers to interact with countrymen from different cantons all across the country. This interaction is to enable cooperation and understanding among all Swiss citizens. What the grid did for me was to force me to interact with others that I would have never, ever approached in my life.

I passed through my teen years with a freedom of thought that my mother never invaded. She spoke so little that I was left to form my own opinions. At least I thought they were my own. It was only later that I realized that I was only parroting ideas I had heard expressed from those in my society who held positions of authority. In my mind people who held positions of authority were teachers, newscasters, journalists, magazine writers, and any other legitimate dispenser of information. I thought that people in each of these groups knew what they were talking about and that they were always right. As an example, if a newscaster announced the results of a study on the benefits of a particular food or drink or certain lifestyle, I believed the study. The newsperson had to be right. He was the authority. I was not. As I followed in the ski tracks of my father, so I followed in the thought tracks of those

in authority.

When I first arrived at Basic, I walked over to an area designated for receiving bunk assignments. A group of four guys, all big and already wearing their army-issued boots and t-shirts, stood nearby. I knew from their accents that they were from Valese, a canton in the southern part of Switzerland where the town of Zermatt lies. I fiddled with my backpack and overheard one of them tell a joke, something crude about a woman and her body parts. Another got in the game and started making fun of a handicapped person, somehow relating the two. The group of guys laughed but I saw nothing funny in what they were saying.

A skinny guy from Basel with a defiant hint of a mustache sauntered up to receive his bunk assignment and stood right beside me as I turned my attention outward, away from the handicap joke.

"No women down in the bunks with us, right?" he asked as he slyly looked around. He declared that the army wasn't a place for women. Announcing that he worked for Swiss Air, he declared that a woman's place was not on the airplane, either. "In the home," he said and repeated, "in the home." He talked about how women should be the ones doing the cooking in the army, not enlisting to do the work of men. I shook my head. My sister was capable of conquering mountains that many men were unable to defeat. Who's to say what women are incapable of doing? I shook my head.

The last to saunter up to our area and receive his bunk assignment was a clean-cut office worker from Bern. He mentioned that he was glad no foreigners would be with us during our training. "In fact," he insisted, "foreign workers shouldn't even be allowed to come to Switzerland. They're only raping our economy, not contributing to it."

I found out later that one of the Valesers, the Baseler, the Berner and I would be placed in the same work group for our eighteen weeks.

In the army these young men, and others I met, regularly and vehemently expressed opinions different from mine. Under normal circumstances I would have never had anything to do with people

like this. These other army inmates certainly weren't persons of authority, yet they disagreed with and made fun of the prevailing thoughts and opinions announced on Switzerland's television and radio stations. These guys were like foreign lands to me. At first I was uncomfortable and bothered. The pressure of the grid and the nuclear cellar was great. It was a testy time. Finally I decided to approach the army and the men it engaged as if they were glaciers to be studied, a mountain range to be conquered.

During Basic I was "the radio guy" in a group being trained to set up radio communication stations. Whatever weekly system we set up had to function properly in all of its details, or we wouldn't get the weekend off. In a real war, aircraft and emergency situations in the mountains would depend on good radio communication. The army wanted us to be ready for that.

Many times during those eighteen weeks my work group had the responsibility of transporting a two hundred pound metal radio box into the mountains. The box was about three feet wide, five feet long and two feet deep. It was awkward to handle, awkward to load into an army vehicle, and awkward to lug into the mountains. But we had to do those things again and again. Sometimes we were lugging and setting up the box in the middle of the night. And sometimes we had to fit the box up and into tight locations. The box seemed to gain weight with each additional incline up the mountains. What was difficult for the weaker and inexperienced guys from Basel and Bern was no problem for the Valeser and me. We had to get the job done, or we wouldn't get the weekend break. The Valeser, the joker, always did the backbreaking work of carrying with no questions asked and no guilt spread around. This made a deep impact on me.

Then one day the Valeser said, "If Switzerland ever goes to war, Switzerland's going to lose, because all the radio guys are going to get crushed by these friggin' radio boxes!"

I laughed.

We all laughed.

And we told that joke often.

I was glad I had opened myself up to the "mountains" because with that came understanding. What I concluded was that in spite of all the personal "junk" the guys who were different from me revealed at the beginning of our eighteen weeks, when the going got tough they were responsible and helpful. I was impressed, and glad I had not let my initial judgment of them close me off to all of their vibrations. Good resided inside of them. Before my army experience, I would have never expected to find it where I did.

During my army time I also became skilled at using a gun, and could accurately shoot at a target more times than not.

Later, after I watched an animal die from a gunshot wound, I learned that shooting at a cardboard target is completely different from shooting at a living thing. If I shot at a shield, it didn't matter if I hit it correctly dead center or not. But not hitting dead center at an animal mattered tremendously to me. Not hitting an animal in the heart meant that he might only be wounded. And if he got away wounded, he would suffer.

I learned something about myself when I had to watch an animal die from a gunshot wound. I learned that if it died from a wound that I had inflicted, I suffered emotionally.

My sense of invincibility had hardened me. The army, of all things, was making me soft again.

ART | BASEL

New surroundings and long marches provide ample opportunities for contemplation, and my thoughts drifted often to my experience at the university in Konstanz. I was overcome with uncertainty each time I considered it. Perhaps I hadn't been exposed to all I needed in order to be a successful practicing artist? Perhaps my insecurity was the fault of the professors who, with their small packages of knowledge, had not filled up my Life Toolbox?

Frequently in the army I assessed my skills and compared them with those of the other guys in my unit. I always came up short in my assessments. It was as if I opened my toolbox, looked inside, and saw a kit three-quarters empty. This is it? I thought.

After Basic Training and returning to Kreuzlingen, I called the National Department of Schools to see if there was the possibility of studying for a Bachelor's or Masters' Degree in Graphic Design in Switzerland.

"Is there a possibility of doing a *Weiterbildung*?" I asked hesitantly. *Weiter* in German means further, and *Bildung* means foundation. I felt I needed a further, more solid foundation.

The Swiss National Department of Schools told me they didn't have such a program, and there wasn't anything interesting in Germany, either.

Programs in Canada and the US were too expensive, so I looked

to England, where I found the Art College of Canterbury.

During a three-months stay in Canterbury I realized that all the students were following the same curriculum I had completed in my four years of study before the army. When the school's director learned that his program was not meeting my needs, he sent me to the Royal College of Art in London. But the Royal College in London was full of rich, spoiled kids who didn't know what they wanted to do with their lives. They were there simply to have a good time, and I wasn't interested in simply having a good time. After staying two days, I boarded a train to the English Channel, caught a ferry to France, and headed home to Switzerland.

On the ferry a Swiss girl and I started up a conversation and half-way through I detailed my recent quest for higher-level design education.

"Did you know there's a Weiterbildung in Basel?" she asked me.

I was flabbergasted. "A Weiterbildung in Basel, Switzerland?"

She nodded her head. "There's a group of teachers who all have the same philosophy of design and they've joined together to teach what they know."

"What do they know?" I asked.

"How to communicate with graphic clarity," she answered. "The government's given them some grants, too, so I don't think the school's too expensive. And I think they're even accepting foreign students. If you go, maybe you'd get a chance to practice your English." Her last comment held more power than she thought.

When I got back to Kreuzlingen, I called the Weiterbildung in Basel. The classes were being offered on selected floors of an Allgemeine Gewerbeschule, or general vocational school, on the east side of town. Even though the administrator told me their time for application was finished, she allowed me to submit my drawings and grades, and after review, accepted me into their program.

I immediately applied for a grant from the federal government since I had used up all of my savings, and was awarded that, too.

Everything fell into place. In the spring of 1977 I moved to Basel.

I had come to believe that at the school in Germany, I was corseted. Actually I had been bound tightly during all of my art school years. The binding existed because of failing to receive any kind of positive reinforcement for my work from the people that counted. Teachers' opinions of my work or worth were inconsequential to me. It was the endorsement from my parents that mattered. Even after the death of my father I still sought his approval. I had only gotten responses from my parents when I did something wrong. So to be loved by them I believed I had to be someone who didn't make any mistakes at all. In school I strove to get good grades. When the good grades failed to produce good responses, I came to the conclusion that I just wasn't good enough. So I kept raising the bar. I kept trying harder and harder. But I never got the reaction I needed. I never got any reaction at all.

Afterward, when I objectively inspected the drawings and designs I had created in Germany, I saw they had no life, no personality. They were like me. I had been bound up like a worm inside a cocoon. Except unlike the worm's cocoon, in my cocoon there was no life.

In Basel I met Armin Hofmann, André Gürtler, Kurt Hauert, Wolfgang Weingart, and others who changed something fundamental in me.

You must understand that the school in Basel was something I chose for myself. Not my father, not my mother, not my sister, not the government. Basel was off the grid.

In Basel there were no grades.

In Basel there were students from all over the world who asked me questions about how I worked and what I thought and how I lived my life.

In Basel I had the time and the freedom to watch how other students worked and I learned new things from them.

In Basel there were teachers who with patience and commitment watched as I tried to solve a drawing or design problem, and allowed me to make mistakes. They did not ignore my attempts. They gave me encouragement as I struggled and fell and picked myself up again.

In Basel, I learned that I did not have to be perfect.

In Basel, unlike in Germany, there were teachers who had worked in business and industry and were not simply academics. I studied packaging with Max Schmidt, an avant-garde designer for Ciba-Geigy, Switzerland's largest pharmaceutical and specialty chemical company. When I experimented with trying to come up with a design for a box for a particular medicine (a task that Mr. Schmidt might have had at Ciba-Geigy), Mr. Schmidt would say, "It's a possible solution, but work on it some more. Perhaps it could be developed into something else, something better." From my work he could foresee a superior solution, but did not solve the problem himself. He pushed me further. He allowed me to be the creator.

I wouldn't say that all of the teachers at the Weiterbildung were the best teachers. In fact, one of them reminded me so much of my father that I had a hard time learning from him. He would berate his adult students if they weren't quick enough. If he thought they were holding their brushes incorrectly, he'd impatiently yank the brushes from their hands and then ask condescendingly, "After all of your years in school you don't know how to hold a brush?" As the ultimate Swiss grid-maker, he insisted that everyone work in the exact manner he did.

Yet there was another teacher who more than made up for all of the imperfections of the terrible one.

Mr. Kurt Hauert, the Weiterbildung's drawing instructor, was a simple, quiet, unassuming man who became well-known and well-liked among all the students in the Gewerbeschule, as well as the Weiterbildung. He impressed upon his students the importance of looking with intention in order to draw an object or a scene well. "You cannot draw unless you *see*," he would say, and patiently helped his students open their eyes. Mr. Hauert would take his own pencil in hand and expertly draw a line here or there over the students' drawings, transforming incorrect perspective and lopsided forms into believable, real shapes in a believable space. But Mr. Hauert never insisted that any student do things exactly his way. He let each one work in his own style.

In Basel my artistic bindings loosened little by little, until after

two years, I was no longer suffocating.

I don't know how Armin Hofmann developed the vision to bring together like-minded teachers in a place like Basel, but I am so grateful he did. He helped me realize that to be a good artist, you must become a real person, a person who does not hide, a person who admits to making mistakes, and a person who thinks his own thoughts.

ART | WORK

After two years in Basel, I started looking through newspaper ads again for a job in Graphic Design. LLP was a well-known advertising company in Switzerland with two offices: one in Basel and one in Zurich. Two guys in Basel, dressed in designer suits and expensive shoes, led me through the interview process. They checked out my jeans and backpack and failed to hide their disdain. Nevertheless, they invited me to the conference room and asked me to sit down. One of them opened up a cigarette box and guided it across the table to me. I did not take a cigarette, and left the box where the smoker had positioned it.

He wrote something in a notebook. I answered questions about my family and my hometown from the smoker, and about my schooling from the other. The smoker kept writing things down in his notebook.

Afterwards I looked around the rest of the workspace. There were thirty or forty people in the Basel office. "You have quite a lot of people working here," I observed out loud.

"Yes, but our office space is large, and it still has a few empty desks, as you can see..." the smoker's voice trailed.

Even so, when LLP Basel offered me a job, I felt that, in that place, there was no space for me. I did not fit.

At Müller-Brockmann Design in Zurich there were six designers, one accountant, two clerks and Mr. Müller-Brockmann. The

owner himself interviewed me. I was a little naïve in those days, and knew only that Mr. Müller-Brockmann was a good graphic designer because I had seen some of his posters. I did not know what other kind of work he was doing. I had no idea he was world-famous.

On the day I met him he wore a turtleneck sweater and blazer and had a nice tan from playing tennis. Although his head was crowned with gray hair, he seemed much younger and healthier than someone in his late sixties.

"Please sit down, Mr. Glauser," he said. I sat opposite him at his desk and began showing him the posters I had designed at the Weiterbildung.

"Ah, yes," he said, "these must have been done under the direction of Mr. Armin Hofmann."

I nodded.

"I know Mr. Hofmann," he said without expression. Then he began to critique each of my posters unmercifully.

The same thing happened when he looked at the product packaging solutions I had devised.

When he turned to my typography layouts, he grunted, "Ah, yes. Wolfgang Weingart. You did these under him, correct?"

I nodded once more.

He picked up one of the layouts. "Nobody can use this, you know. No client would pay for anything like this."

I...I didn't know what to say. He took the wind out of me and I didn't have the strength to defend any of my work. I waited helplessly as he carefully studied each sample of my work before turning to the next page of my portfolio.

Are you bound to this kind of design?" he finally asked.

I was naïve, but I was not stupid. I knew Mr. Müller-Brockmann was a very good designer, and unlike the people at LLP who were doing only advertising, Müller-Brockmann was doing DESIGN work in general. I wanted to do DESIGN work, and I did need a job. Unless he turns out to be a jerk, I'll be able to learn something from him, or at least from the people in his studio, I thought. He

had criticized my work, but yet he had studied it, and I felt that if I had had the words to explain it, then perhaps he would have accepted it.

"No, I am always ready to learn a new way," I answered.

For the first time, Mr. Müller-Brockmann gave me a hint of a smile and began to talk about his approach to design.

"Look at it," he commanded as he pointed to my chair.

I looked.

The bottom part was made of metal. Above it there was a wicker back of woven wood. "There are some principles of design you must always keep in mind. If you ignore them, you will fail." He tapped the seat. "The seat is of metal, the backing of wood. You cannot put two materials together without having a neutral material in-between. Rubber is neutral, and look, there are tubes of rubber placed in-between the metal and the wood."

He paused, touched his forefinger and thumb to his chin, and went on. "Specific lettertypes, or fonts, have a function. You can't arbitrarily mix one font up with another because, if you do, you will deny the function of both. Besides not mixing them up improperly, you must handle lettertypes carefully, using correct spacing and sizing, because the whole point of letters is to form words---to communicate. Letters ought to be arranged so that words and sentences can be read easily. By their arrangement of letterforms, or letters, some designers make words harder to read than is necessary. Others make them impossible to read."

Müller-Brockmann heaved a sigh of relief when I nodded my head in agreement. I believe he was looking for a sign. He was, afterall, spending an unusual amount of time with me.

After this mini-lecture he showed me around the office, and never once asked me any personal questions.

I later found out that Müller-Brockmann was at odds with Mr. Hofmann because he thought that Mr. Hofmann purposely organized a Gewerbeschule in Basel to compete with a Gewerbeschule in Zurich that Müller-Brockmann himself wanted to head up. But Mr. Hofmann was not competing with Mr. Müller-Brockmann. Mr. Hofmann had only set up his international

design program at the Gewerbeschule in Basel, he did not run the Gewerbeschule. For some reason, Mr. Müller-Brockmann ignored this minor detail.

It was Müller-Brockmann's style to belittle artists at the beginning of his relationships with them, probably in order to instill fear in them. He wanted them to fear him so that they'd trust *his* design style and not their own. I later came to believe that he acted this way because he himself was afraid. He was afraid that if he didn't criticize first he might end up seeing the really good work of others. If he saw the really good work of others, then he'd have to question his own, and he'd discover *that he might have to change.* His approach to design was based on a grid system that was certainly trustworthy and produced designs that "held up", but it was formulaic and predictable, leaving little room for unexpected visual delights. Mr. Müller-Brockmann was an excellent grid-maker, yet he may have become stuck in his own grids.

When I left the offices of MBD the day of my interview, I had come to the conclusion that Mr. Müller-Brockmann was very narrow-minded, and that there was no chance he'd offer me a job. But while I was in class three days later, he called at my pensión and left a message saying I should return his call, no matter what time in the evening I retrieved it. I arrived home after eleven o'clock that night, and because of his message, returned the call then.

"If you're still interested in working with me," he said, "let's talk about a day you can come by and we can discuss the contract." He never explained why he changed his mind and found my work good enough for him to offer me a job.

I ended up working with Müller-Brockmann Design for three years, and during that time was given a lot of good, challenging projects. We had no computers then, but everything Müller-Brockmann Design did was technical. Mr. Müller-Brockmann was a mathematician as well as an artist. He strove to bring different elements together creatively, but made sure the mathematical relationships among the various parts was accounted for. He was constantly evaluating the size of the shape to the amount of the

space to size of type. For instance, if we were doing a layout and the type was bordering a square, the size of the type had to relate to the size of the square in a mathematical way. In my own work, I was always required to explain how each thing balanced the next. I had to verbalize it. I had to justify the choices I made for my finished products.

When Mr. Müller-Brockmann realized that I understood letter-spacing and saw that I was willing to be detailed, he encouraged me. When he saw that I, too, enjoyed working conceptually, bringing different elements together to make them work relationally, I earned his trust. I believe that it was because of my willingness, at the beginning, to follow in his tracks that Mr. Müller-Brockmann became positive and encouraging with me, and allowed me eventual freedom.

The experience of working in this small design office was so different from what the rest of my life experience had been before Basel, especially with my father. Besides being encouraged and receiving positive feedback in whatever design I attempted, I was forced to communicate verbally. I was never made to feel stupid.

I worked similarly to my boss, whom I was eventually granted the privilege of calling Seppli, a shortened version of Josef. I worked similarly, but was not as bound as he was. The Weiterbildung had loosened me. I used the Grid System to expand my design possibilities (as Wolfgang Weingart had taught) while Seppli used the Grid System to cut down his possibilities. I think he was afraid of losing himself to a universe of possibilities.

You can become crazy if you go outside the Grid and don't know which way to go. But if you stay within it you can also become too predictable and stale.

In the city, if you always walk or drive the same road to get to a certain destination, of course you always know where you are and always know how to get to where you want to go. But always driving the same way never lets you become aware of what alternate routes exist to reach your destination. And who knows? Maybe an alternate route is more scenic, faster, more interesting, more challenging, provides more options than the first or lets you know you might want to be doing something completely different

with your time. Seppli might have seen different ways to solve a problem, but only within his System, never deviating far from Highway One.

I learned not long ago that in my every day life, in my design work, and in the sculpting that I do, that I come up with really nice results by just doing things in the moment, and doing them quickly. Working this way gives me great relief. This is a part of myself that before Alaska I never allowed. Everything always had to be done while in control. Everything always had to be done a certain way. I recognize that I must keep to some structure if I am working on communication design. This type of art has a function: to communicate a specific message. But if I am just expressing myself, making "art," then I can be very free and the possibilities are endless.

It took me some time to come away from the Grid, to figure out another system that I could work within.

I began thinking about how to structure chaos, and started looking all around me at the things that appear to have no systems whatsoever to them.

As a child I occasionally came upon chaos spider webs and was always fascinated by them. They were complete messes! How could the creators of these messes ever figure out what they were doing? How could a spider use parts of a plant jutting out into his creation and end up with anything workable? As a child I figured that the spider must have just gone crazy. That it must have fallen on its head. Otherwise, what it created would have had much more structure and organization to it. Did it set out to create a mess? Or did it set out to create something much more shapely and end up with a mess? I couldn't figure it out.

With each passing year I looked more carefully and observed that although each web was different, each was similar to the next. Each one was individually built, and each individual spider had developed a system. A spider fixes a thread to a plant, and the plant is then integrated into the structure of the web. As an adult peering closely into a chaos web thickly constructed on a shrub, I discovered definite forms and three-dimensional geometric shapes. Through the crossing of threads, the shapes repeat themselves,

revealing a system. I began to revel in discovering the structures within each messy shrub web I came across.

I have come to enjoy Chaos Stories as well. These are stories without endings. The authors of these stories give their readers a lot of freedom in imagining different endings. I have found that these kinds of stories open up the possibility of coming up with new ways of thinking.

For me the Grid is a guideline. I look at the crosspoints of the Grid as question marks --- question marks that force me to ask which way to go. Maybe the chaos spider looks at a branch or a leaf as a question mark, too, and then continues on, creating a structure of forms within forms.

I'm curious all the time. Presently I have a computer screen in front of me, but I want to see what's behind it. I'm always wanting to do a *Weiterbildung*. To go further. That is one reason I went to Alaska.

THE CALL OF THE WILD

The first time I set foot in the upper regions of North America was with my sister, Kathrin.

I had been with Müller-Brockmann Design for two years when Kathrin invited me to join her on a trip to the wheat farm of a school friend who had emigrated to Grand Prairie, Alberta, in Canada. The farm happened to be near many Blackfoot and Cree Indian historical sites, which we were curious to explore. I couldn't help but be overwhelmed at the immensity of the space around those sites. I stood on land that stretched out into the distance so far that I could see where it melded into the sky. I tried to imagine what it was like being a Blackfoot Indian, whose home this was so many years ago. He was not lost on the plains. The plains were his living room, the sky his domed ceiling, and the grasses blowing in the breeze his living room rug. Everything was so big, so grand, so separate from civilization, and so separate from other human beings.

The whispering plains stirred memories that had been locked up in darkened prisons of my soul, forbidden to show themselves. When a whisper wrested open one small cell, the memory of my marmot escaped. With it quickly came a picture of Reguli waving good-bye at the train station, giving me a red paper rose. "This is for when you come back," she said.

I stood on those Canadian plains feeling an ache --- an ache to return to the wilderness and the aloneness of my childhood.

I had tried to do that as an adult in Switzerland, but found that wherever I went there were too many people. Switzerland had become too small.

Now the plains awakened the desire again. They were calling me to return to the wilderness. Why? What had I lost there? What did I need to find?

Was God calling me to meet him? Was it there that I could shake my fist at him and show him I was the one in control of my life? That I really was invincible? That even his Nature in all its wildness couldn't conquer me like it conquered my father?

I believed that whatever I could possibly encounter in the wild, I would remember how to see and feel with all my senses ... and survive, because I would be prepared. I would remember how to see and feel with all my senses...unlike my father...who was not prepared...on his last day.

I knew I would return.

Back in Switzerland, I realized that what my inner being demanded was not just a summer dalliance on the plains of Canada. My childhood visions returned and they called me into the mountains, into the cold, into the snow. A desire began to burn inside of me to go one step further than the plains of Canada I had just visited. In my mind, Alaska was one step further, and one step closer to the wilderness the visions spoke of. The visions were a call of the wild.

For all the sensible members among my family, friends and coworkers, I knew I needed a reasonable explanation for my "crazy" Year-In-Alaska Plan. (The Plan called for a timeframe of at least a year...because the challenge wouldn't be complete if I didn't experience every season.)

Alaska would be "Off the Grid" for Mr. Müller-Brockmann. What would I tell him?

Around the office I began thinking out loud.

"What would it be like," I wondered, "to pitch a tent on the tundra of Alaska and wake to the cawing of a bald-headed eagle? What amazing photographs or drawings of the animals that lived in the mountain forests could a person create? If I embarked on

such an adventure, could I really endure every season? Could I endure even one Alaskan winter, known for its brief hours of sunlight? Could anyone really survive that?"

I assured my boss that if anyone could do it, I could.

My childhood and the army had prepared me.

White-water rafting and mountaineering in my homeland had become too tame for me. In Switzerland, a person is never farther away from food or shelter than a day trip. I needed more. I didn't speak of my visions, only of "dreams" of being completely alone in wide-open spaces, inhabited only by wildlife.

"Where will you live exactly?" he asked.

"I can't make precise plans from here about where I'll stay," I told him, "because things always turn out differently from what you expect."

This would be one of those cross points on the Grid. A question mark. Müller-Brockmann wasn't very comfortable with that statement, so I tried to reassure him. "I know I want to canoe somewhere in the summer, and I want to spend the winter in the mountains."

He sighed. He was probably thinking that he had given me too much Grid freedom.

When I told my mother I wanted to spend a year in the wilderness in Alaska, she was hiding in her turtle shell. In fact, since she lived there regularly, I did not expect an emotional reaction. Or even a verbal one. I missed having a human, natural response from her. I knew, though, when I told her about Alaska, that she was afraid I wouldn't come back. It was something I felt more than saw, because her face was a mask.

Some of my friends found the idea of my going to Alaska intriguing. Most thought I was going just to die. They joked that I would be making quite an effort to commit suicide.

A few thought that I was just crazy.

And, of course, I was.

But craziness is not all bad. There is a big range to craziness. There is a constructive craziness as well as a destructive craziness.

I'm glad there are a lot of crazy people in the world because craziness changes a lot of things for the good. I think my plan was in the constructive range, because it would become a well-developed plan --- a well-developed plan that would take me through a whole year.

There were a few people who talked about joining me. They were ones with whom I figured I could make such a trip. But work or family responsibilities prevented them from being away from Switzerland for a full year.

The fact was that I had become very comfortable with the idea of going alone, although I did consider taking a dog.

In the end I did not take a dog, but neither did I go alone.

In the end I found a human traveling companion.

I did not choose him.

He chose me.

I was a member of a sports and white-water rafting club near Lucerne, and at the beginning of February of the year I turned twenty-eight years old, I began telling people at the club that I would be leaving soon for Alaska. I wasn't bragging. I needed to let the club know that my membership would be on hold for quite some time.

Tobias came to me after he had heard the news from his brother, a member of the same sports club. Tobias asked me about my plans. I told him of my desire to live in the wilderness for one full year, through all the seasons. I told him about the activities I planned to occupy myself with, and I told him I didn't know how it would end. I told him I had a lot of fortitude to persevere, and assured him that I did not intend to commit suicide.

Tobias asked if he could join me.

Now *I* was the one to look at *him* a little strangely. I admitted to him that I could get lost out there, that he should consider that.

He shrugged his shoulders. "I guess that's a possibility," he said.

I suggested that Tobias and I take some canoe trips together. Didn't I need to give him some kind of test? I wanted to see first hand what kind of survival skills he had. He was a nice guy

who dressed conservatively in khaki pants and sweater vests. He appeared much too coddled, protected, and untested.

On the first canoe trip Tobias remained very reserved. He listened to what I had to say, but would not share any ideas --- about anything. He had no stories to tell. The only bit of news he offered was that he had never had a girlfriend.

After our second trip I still wasn't sure Tobias could handle being in the mountains alone in Switzerland, let alone in the barren mountains of a far-off land where he had only himself to depend on for survival.

Then Tobias invited me to his home for dinner.

His mother met me at the door. If she had had a shotgun when I entered the house she would have pointed it at me and pulled the trigger without thinking. In her eyes I saw the accusation: "You're the one! You're the one who's going to kill my baby! If you take him *you* will be responsible!" From that point on Mrs. Ghertli talked so fast and so loud, Tobias couldn't come to words. She talked about everything that was nothing, going on and on about how hard it was to get things out of the garden, how cold the weather had been, how the neighbors were too loud or too secretive, how no one did any work around the house except her. Life was one big STRESS for her. If it were possible, her sharp nose and cheekbones became even more so as the evening wore on. Nothing in her softened.

Tobias' father remained wordless until Mrs. Ghertli left the table to bring the dessert.

Mr. Ghertli had grown up in the mountains and asked me if I had ever heard of his childhood village. "The family often goes up there," he said in a low voice, "and we were thinking that we'd move to the mountains when I retire." Tobias's mother returned to the dining room and the subject was dropped. When Mrs. Ghertli began complaining about a local politician, Mr. Ghertli loosened up and joined in. He added further complaints about the company for which he worked, a company that specialized in food-canning.

"It doesn't function economically," he emphasized. He was rewarded by a pause in the conversation from his wife.

"It's my boss's fault, or maybe it's his boss's fault. I'm just a middle-management guy," he admitted, and glanced at his wife. "I'm afraid ---" I think he was going to say that he was afraid he was going to lose his job, but his wife cut him off.

"Did you see how much the monastery has raised its bread prices?"

Neither parent approached the subject of our Alaska trip. Neither one asked, "What are your plans? What do you intend to do there every day?" That would have made a nice conversation.

Tobias never relaxed for one minute during that dinner. His mother admonished him for not taking the potatoes, for holding his fork incorrectly and for never having anything to say. I saw the food get caught in Tobias' throat.

That night as I looked at him across the tidy little table with neat bowls of beans and potatoes and cheese and chicken, I saw nobody there. Nobody was home.

I knew that night that Tobias needed to take some trip, any trip, to get away from this house. He needed to extricate himself from this chaos web that was suffocating him. Why not use my Alaska trip to do what he needed to do?

After my visit to the house of Tobias Ghertli, the mother called me once by phone. She screamed at me that I was taking away her son. She screamed in my ear that I was going to kill him.

I answered firmly that her son was twenty-two years old, and ready to make his own choices and decisions.

The mother phoned me that one and only time. She apparently sensed I would have no more of her.

PREPARING FOR ALASKA

My normal strengthening routine included weekly time-frames for jogging. I jogged every evening for about six miles. Sometimes, if I was in the right frame of mind, I jogged twice that amount. Every other weekend I would run up the trails at Üetliberg, a small mountain on the west side of Zurich. There are a series of stairs at Elefantenbach Tobel, a ravine on the eastern side of Zurich, and when I wasn't at Üetliberg I would sprint up and down the stairs until my legs couldn't move. Also on the schedule were weight-lifting and mountaineering, for building strength as well as endurance.

Tobias started serious training because I suggested it. Our two canoe trips had been passable and pleasant, but I discovered quickly that Tobias needed to get much stronger if he meant to keep up with me in the wilderness. Tobias was in the habit of jogging, playing soccer, walking and hiking, but I felt he needed to do much more serious training. He said he would. He never did go mountaineering with me in Switzerland, but he should have. People think that everyone in Switzerland is a good skier, but that isn't so. Tobias wasn't a good skier. I found that out later, after I had already committed to have him come along with me. But I didn't worry too much about his intermediate skiing skills. I thought I could teach him. We would have time. If we made it to the winter.

Books written in English about the Klondike Gold Rush and

climbing Mt. McKinley made their way into my library, next to army survival books that taught me how to build outdoor shelters as well as fires after a week of rain.

In Switzerland I only found one book regarding edible plants in Alaska, but held out hope that we'd learn more once we reached our destination.

Two years before leaving for Alaska, I experienced two serendipities.

The first came about because of an ad in a Zurich newspaper regarding a room available for rent in a house on the shore of Lake Zurich. The proprietor was a medical doctor who had traveled extensively, spending a considerable amount of time in Africa. In fact, she had developed a sickness there that affected her brain. I didn't know this until I had signed a renter's agreement and was committed to stay for a year.

Frau Dr. Hugentobler continued her medical practice in Zurich while I lived in her home, but I often had to take care of her. She had no relatives in the city, and I came to feel responsible for her.

When I remained longer at work or spent some hours away training, Frau Dr. Hugentobler would call me and ask, "Where are you, Ruedi? When will you be home?" She was afraid to be by herself.

But I was willing to make sacrifices regarding Frau Dr. Hugentobler because living with her did come with benefits. Her ample house on the lake included a beautiful garden and the rent was cheap. Ultimately I was saving money for my Alaska expedition.

I think Frau Dr. Hugentobler's way of thanking me was by generously offering to support me in any way she could regarding my trip to the forty-ninth state.

She convinced me that because I would regularly be using an axe and sharp knives in Alaska, there was great danger of being cut accidently and often. She suggested it would be good to know how to close wounds and handle infections. She insisted that I learn how to stitch up wounds with a surgical needle, and used threads made from dried and treated intestines of a cow or sheep from

Argentina, sometimes known as catgut, to teach me.

Frau Dr. Hugentobler recommended that I take with me to Alaska two different kinds of threads: one for internal wounds that would dissolve, and the second for the outside of wounds that would have to be manually removed.

Human skin grows in three layers, and each layer possesses a different quality. The outermost layer, called the epidermis, is soft and rather elastic. This waterproof layer is what protects you from the elements and gives you your skin tone. Underneath the epidermis is the dermis, where tougher connective tissue, nerve fibers, blood capillaries, and hair follicles show themselves. Deeper down you can find a leather-like layer intermixed with muscle.

I practiced suturing "cuts" on rubber balls made especially for medical interns. In fact, Frau Dr. Hugentobler allowed me, outfitted in a white lab coat and looking very official, to fill in as her medical intern at the office.

One day an older gentleman came in because of a deep gash to his leg.

"I'm training my intern on performing sutures," Frau Dr. Hugentobler explained to the gentleman. "Would you be agreeable in allowing him (here she pointed to me) to practice on you?"

The old man looked me over. "Hmpf," he said, then studied my white coat. "Fine," he concluded.

And so I performed my first, live, suturing job. Sewing skin together is not easy, by the way. Don't let anyone tell you it is. The biggest challenge is to knot the thread and make it hold.

The most difficult job is always to make something last.

A second serendipity was making the acquaintance of a butcher in Zurich who offered to show me how to kill and efficiently cut apart a large animal. Such a skill might be necessary in order to survive a harsh winter in the hinterlands of Alaska.

One Thursday evening the butcher invited me into his shop where a live cow waited patiently in a steel stall.

"Take hold of the metal bolt gun, place it on the head of the animal," the butcher directed, "then press the button."

I pressed. There was no loud sound, and no blood appeared. Yet the cow dropped dead to the ground anyway from the impact of the metal bolt. It was a sickening feeling to see him crumble upon himself. I felt it in my belly and found myself apologizing to the animal.

"You'll have to slit the cow's throat so that the blood can drain," the butcher continued matter-of-factly as he moved toward some leather straps hanging from the ceiling.

"But first let's tie up the back legs to hang the animal upside down. This'll let the blood flow into the bucket."

After slitting the throat, I proceeded to open the underside of the belly and cut out the organs. When you cut open a recently killed animal, fluid and waste from around the animal's digestive track come out and there's quite a putrid smell. At that time the butcher and I wore no hair or facemasks, and the odor from the mixture of blood, meat, fluid and feces was nauseating.

The butcher gathered up the intestines used for making sausage, bagged them and stored them in the refrigerated area of his shop.

"We'll disconnect the head next," the butcher said when he returned. "I get good money for the tongue, but I don't need anything else from the head."

After disposing of the skull, I had to cut above the hooves to separate the cow's skin from its body. You must use a fine knife to release the skin because the butcher also sells the skin. A cleanly cut skin commands more money than one hacked off hurriedly.

The penultimate step was to cut the body in half, from top to bottom, through the sternum of the rib cage.

Each half would hang in a very cold refrigerator for a designated time in order to age the beef. Aging beef develops additional tenderness and flavor. So every ten days to six weeks the body halves would be rotated to the front of the refrigerator and then onto a chopping block.

The butcher hung the animal we had cut and removed an aged half-cow. After loosening this aged half-cow's limbs at their joints, we cut the meat apart.

The whole process didn't calm me or give me confidence, even though I was now prepared to butcher a large animal. It unnerved me. Just thinking about what I would do if I had an injured or dead moose in front of me made my stomach turn.

Still, I thought I might have to kill a moose for survival. And even though the circumstances would never be as controlled as they were at the butcher's (there would be no steel stall to keep an animal in place, no harness to upend the moose so that all the blood could run out), I knew I was good at adapting. I was good at making something out of nothing. If in Alaska I needed to kill a moose but didn't have a pulley, I figured I'd be able to find a way to cut and drain the animal properly.

But I wondered if I would be able to even complete the first step in the process. Shooting a moose with a bullet so that it will die is very difficult. You have to be a very good hunter. And anyway, I didn't like the idea of shooting an animal which I might not immediately kill. Maybe it would run and hide where I couldn't find it. It would suffer, and as I learned in the army, I would suffer.

Tobias was the one who eventually bought a lightweight, 20-gauge Remington shotgun. "In case the wild animals get too... close," he said.

I remained ambivalent about carrying a gun.

With a gun anyone could be fooled into thinking he was safe and nothing could harm him.

But what would happen if the shot from his gun only managed to wound an animal? Wouldn't he be worse off? Wouldn't he have to further defend himself against a frightened, angry, and very unpredictable beast?

My choice was to depend upon my wits and my body to escape the snare of any wild creature.

After all, wasn't I invincible?

SUPPLIES, A DIARY, & A BOOK

As the days came nearer for departure, I set aside the following clothes and supplies I would pack in my luggage:

1 Pair Wool Trousers

1 Pair Mountaineering Boots (sturdier than regular hiking boots)

3 Pairs Wool Socks

3 Pairs Underwear

3 T-shirts

I Pair Sneakers

1 Rain Jacket

1 Wool Sweater

1 Pair Wool Mittens

1 Wool Cap

1 Tooth Brush + 1 Tube of Toothpaste

1 Comb

0 Shaving Supplies (no need because of my beard)

1 Bar of Body Soap (scent-free)

1 Tent

1 Swiss Army Knife (not huge, but one that included a saw and scissors)

300 Waterproof Matches (stored in 6 empty film roll containers)

1 Rollei Camera (35mm) + 40 Rolls of Slide Film

1 First-Aid Kit

1 Survival Kit

Frau Dr. Hugentobler helped me put together the First-Aid Kit. She was the one who wrote the prescriptions and suggested the dosages and amounts of medicines I should take with me.

The First Aid Kit included:

10 Doses of Dafalgan (a painkiller, intended for emergency use only; not to be used for ordinary headaches)

1 Box of Band-Aids (large; to be cut up as needed)

1 Small Bottle of High-Concentration Merfen (similar to mercurochrome, for use on wounds to prevent bacterial infections)

1 Tourniquet Band (to prevent loss of life even at the cost of a limb; daily we'd be working with an axe; cutting a limb could easily happen)

2 Tubes of Tooth Fixative (in case of cavities)

1 Package Immodium (in case of diarrhea)

1 Space Blanket (an extremely light, compact piece of survival gear used to retain body warmth)

50 Waterproof Matches (protected in a 35mm film roll container)

Thread + Needles (to stitch up wounds)

Scissors

Tweezers

Scalpel

Gauze

Paper + Pencil

The Space Blanket especially impressed me, and I felt lucky to have it. Made from a thin sheet of plastic coated with very precise amounts of pure aluminum vapor, it weighed no more than a few ounces, yet it could carry a one-hundred-eighty pound human body. Wrapped inside, a person could retain up to eighty percent of his or her radiated body heat. The Space Blanket's composition was known as mylar, a material first developed in 1964 for the US

Space Program.

The supplies for the Survival Kit, which I intended to carry around my waist at all times, included:

1 Fish Hook

20 Twenty-Foot Lengths of Yarn (for fishing)

50 Waterproof Matches (protected in one 35mm film roll container)

1 Penknife (a small folding pocket knife)

1 Space Blanket (folded into a 4"x3" rectangle)

Tobias also packed:

Woolen Clothes

1 Small First-Aid Kit (included band-aids, gauze, merfen, and blister bandages for his feet)

1 Survival Kit (I gave him my list for this)

We planned to protect our Survival Kits in waterproof packs and keep them clipped to our waists at all times. Both of us were well-aware of the ease with which we could lose our backpacks downstream from fast water or a canoe tip. Plus rain, or even paddle splashes, could dampen all of our supplies. So keeping our Survival Kits dry and clipped to our waists at all times was of utmost importance.

Other things like a canoe, paddles, life vests, supply sleds, and mosquito spray we planned on purchasing in Alaska. I had read about the Alaskan mosquitoes and knew we were going to need some super-power protection, so we planned to buy a brand that was illegal to sell in Switzerland. And no doubt we'd buy a cooking pot and pan, plus some type of concentrated non-polluting, fragrance-free liquid laundry soap. (Fragrances attract bears, who are ever-curious about what "that fine smell" is and are quick to follow their noses to the source of the smell!) For the winter we would need to buy our skis, plus other things that we'd find out about when we got to Alaska.

In my luggage I also packed a diary and a book. The diary was

one hundred pages of plain white paper in a standard European A-4 notebook size. I planned to write and draw in pencil, which, I knew if dampened, wouldn't get washed away.

The book I carried with me was *2001, A Space Odyssey*. At the time I wasn't able to explain to anyone why I included it, except that I was very impressed by the movie when it was first released. The way the movie was made fascinated me. It was the first science-fiction movie I had ever seen, and everything seemed very plausible. In my mind I would have made the spaceship exactly like Stanley Kubrick had created it.

When *2001, A Space Odyssey* was written, a human being had not yet even set foot on the moon. Yet here the characters in the book were, already exploring a planet further away from earth than the moon. They were on a flight to Jupiter, a brand new frontier.

In Alaska I would be exploring a new frontier, too.

The book's characters needed courage to move out into space, not knowing how their journey would end, and I needed courage to move out into the vast state of Alaska, not knowing how my exploration would end, either.

Paragraph by paragraph I read it.

And after finishing it, I left it out there in the Alaskan wilderness, in a tiny library where I discovered other books that were to affect me much more profoundly than *2001, A Space Odyssey*.

ALASKA

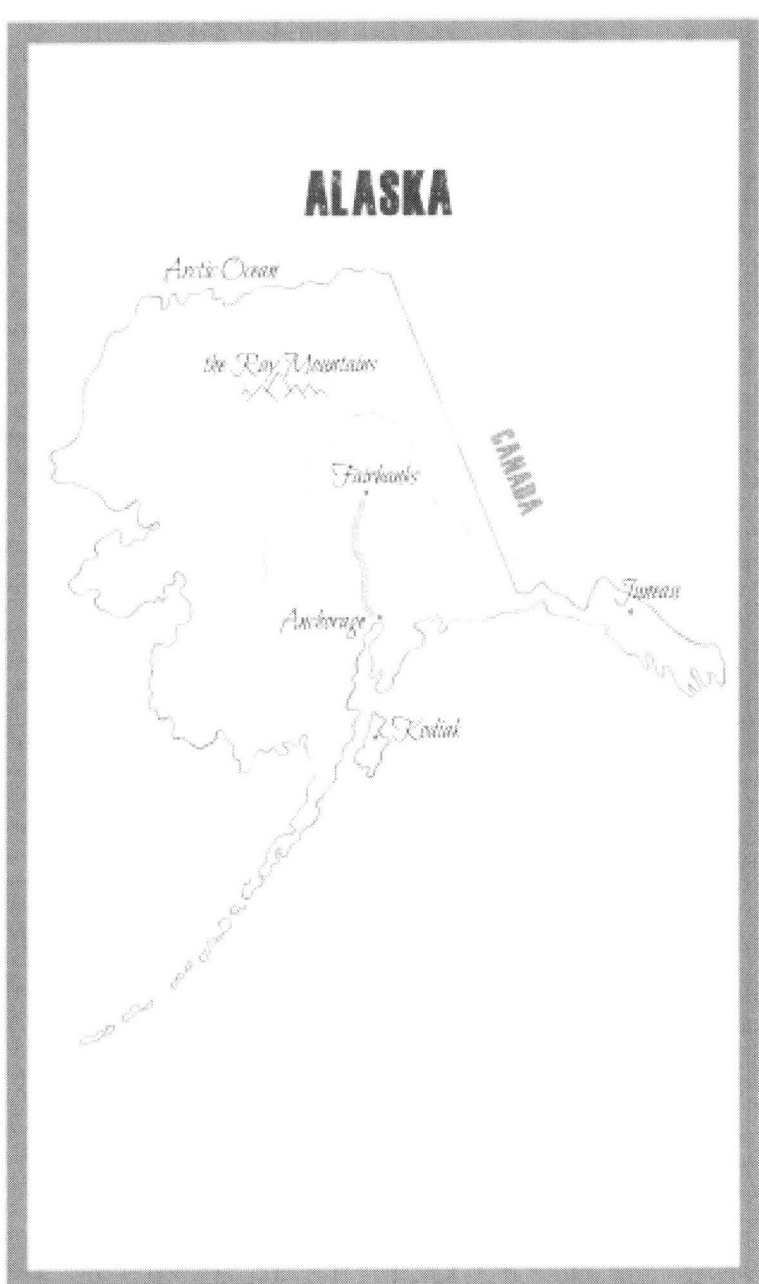

| 12 |

ANCHORAGE-BOUND

For a year-long stay in Alaska I budgeted ten thousand Swiss Francs (which at that time was the equivalent of roughly five thousand US dollars). The biggest expense was the airline ticket with SAS, which swallowed up four thousand Swiss Francs (two thousand dollars). The ticket came with a high price tag because it needed to be "open-ended", since I had not decided on a return date.

In May of my twenty-eighth year my sister, Kathrin, drove Tobias and me from Kreuzlingen to the airport in Zurich.

On the flight I wore a T-shirt, jeans, sneakers and my Survival Kit wrapped in plastic inside a leather fanny pack buckled around my waist. All of the other possessions I had gathered and packed for the trip lay below me, in the belly of the airplane. If the luggage got lost, Tobias and I just might have to turn around and go back home.

We flew from Zurich to Stockholm, Sweden, and then from Stockholm to Anchorage, Alaska. Our luggage arrived with us after all.

Before leaving Switzerland, at the US Embassy in Bern, I had requested a twelve-month visa, nine months longer than the US typically allowed for its tourists. But the US wasn't making any exceptions.

I was not worried, though. Americans are nice people, I figured,

and I was convinced that if I just talked with someone at Passport Control in Alaska, then that someone would be willing to stamp my (and Tobias') passport with permission to stay at least one year.

Upon arriving in Anchorage, Tobias and I approached the immigration booth. I cleared my throat to speak. English. Now I speak English, I told myself.

"Um, excuse me. Um, we'd like to stay in Alaska for a year. We hope that is possible."

The burly immigration officer shifted in his chair and crossed his arms over a crooked tie. He didn't say anything.

"Can you please stamp our passports to allow us to stay for a full year?" I asked again, not wanting my request to be misunderstood. The officer took our passports, pushed them to the edge of his desk, and told us to take a seat by the wall at the back of his booth. We sat. The whole time we sat, those passports lay where they had been pushed. For an hour we waited and the officer never once picked them up. After an hour the man in the booth leaned over one of the passports and called out, "Mr. Glauser!"

Tobias and I approached the booth.

Mr. Officer theatrically stamped both passports, then told us we could go.

Walking away from the booth we studied the stamps. They gave us permission to stay for one month only --- not even the three months that are usual for tourists! Tobias gave me a sideways glance. I read the question in it: Is this the beginning of a failed trip, Ruedi, because you, who thought you could control everything, could not even control the first thing?

So I headed immediately to the immigration office in town. There we met a nice lady who was happy to welcome two European boys to Alaska. She arranged everything so that we were awarded a visa for one and a half years. When you go directly to places of authority and speak to the people in charge, they are often very open. Something good almost always happens.

In Anchorage I tried to open a bank account, but to open a bank account in Alaska I needed a Social Security number. I also needed a Social Security number to get a driver's license. But in order to

get a Social Security number I needed to be a US citizen, which I was not. What to do?

Tobias and I made our way to the Social Security office in Fairbanks where we met another nice lady who looked to be in her thirties and who, like us, was dressed in jeans and a long-sleeve shirt. She seemed to understand my dilemma immediately and, from the comfort of her desk chair, called in from the adjoining office another woman who entered the room and sat on the desk's edge. Together they discussed how to issue me a Social Security number. They spoke in low voices to each other, then got up and moved around the office, checking through folders in this or that cabinet. While they were figuring out what to do, they offered Tobias and me tea. I heard one of the women say under her breath to the other, "Just give him a number from a dead guy." Eventually they found a Canadian number I could use. Or so they said. In any case, with the number they issued me, I was able to open a bank account in Alaska to deposit my cash, and also to have additional money from Switzerland deposited into the account, if necessary.

Afterward on the street Tobias pulled from his pocket a slip of paper that had on it the name of a Swiss guy named Tomas Wyrsch. Tomas was a friend of a friend of a friend who lived on the outskirts of Anchorage. We found and knocked on his door. He was very happy to see us.

Tomas Wyrsch had already lived many years in the United States, had become a US citizen, had worked on the Alaskan pipeline, and had even been in the US army. After his stint in the army, Tomas continued to reside in Anchorage, founded a construction business, figuring that the Anchorage population and economy would grow. He bought land, built a house and other buildings on the land, and then sold what he owned. Tomas had been a metal-worker --- trained in Switzerland to mold iron. In Anchorage he was building beautiful Swiss-crafted brick houses, and adorning them with artistic iron railings. He was prospering.

Tomas told us that while living in Alaska a few years before, he had put an ad in a Swiss magazine seeking a wife. And so he found one, much younger than he. She traveled from Alsace-Lorraine --- a small piece of land bordering France, Germany and Switzerland

--- to live with Tomas in Alaska. Her name was Elise. Tomas and Elise now had two small children and lived in one of the houses he had built. He invited us to stay with him for a few days before we left on the train for Fairbanks.

We hiked the nearby wilderness together, and Tomas pointed out Earthquake Park, explaining that it had been "created" during the 1964 earthquake when part of Anchorage fell into the sea.

"That was a massive earthquake," he said. "The second-most-powerful earthquake in recorded history. It was a magnitude of 9.2. A lot of coastal villages were destroyed. Lucky for us the center was far enough away from Anchorage that it killed less than 150 people. It could have killed thousands."

I knew the Aleutian Islands that belong to Alaska were littered with volcanoes, but I never considered that I could be caught in an earthquake in Alaska. An earthquake would just have to be one more thing that would be on my list to confront.

Tomas Wyrsch, who didn't like the cold at all, told us we were crazy guys because we had come to live in the Alaskan cold. "During the winter," he said, my family and I fly to Hawaii."

Tomas was also surprised that at the moment I was refusing to eat meat.

"Up here, everyone eats meat. You have to eat meat to stay healthy."

Before visiting the butcher in Zurich I had considered the possibility of becoming a vegetarian, and the actual experience of killing a cow pushed me over the edge. I continued eating fish, though, and getting my protein requirements from fish seemed to be perfectly adequate for me. If it came about during the winter that I would have to kill a moose in order to survive...well, I would decide what to do about a moose when the time came.

Anchorage is the largest city in Alaska, but Tobias and I were easily able to traverse the town on foot. Nevertheless, there were few helpful signs to direct us, and few cheerful shops and restaurants to welcome us in. Only a scattering of buildings stood taller than a story or two high, and only some of those were constructed of brick. The rest looked as if they had been quickly

assembled from untreated lumber.

Quite a few of the wooden houses had been sprayed with thick insulation --- the kind of insulation that expands after being applied and makes a structure look like a doughboy. It's a cheap way to insulate a house, but not very attractive, or lasting. After a few years the elements eat away at the "dough," leaving the marshmallow shapes pockmarked and covered in soot.

You don't see the coast from downtown Anchorage, although Cook Inlet is within an hour's walking distance.

Tobias and I walked everywhere, in spite of the fact that there were neither sidewalks nor crosswalks, except of course right in the center of town. The center of town housed the tourist office, the Post Office and a few more government buildings, some eateries, and a few small museums. We had to walk on the same part of the road on which people drove their cars. Luckily for us few cars occupied the roads, no matter the time of day.

The population of Anchorage was mostly American, mostly men, and mostly bearded men! There was talk everywhere about building a second pipeline for natural gas, and these men had honed in on Anchorage so they could be first in line for the new pipeline jobs.

Many of the men I met there had fought in Vietnam. Some had lost a hand or an eye in the war --- and it was evident that most had been mentally, emotionally, or spiritually damaged by it. They were withdrawn, and backed away from attention, bright lights, fast cars, fast women...and responsibility. A few told me they were in Alaska because they just wanted to live in peace. The residents of Anchorage seemed to understand that. The men were accepted, not judged.

What disquieted Tobias and me the most in Anchorage was coming across ghostlike creatures who often wandered aimlessly around town. The first time we saw one it unsettled us. Then, the more we saw, the more distraught and saddened we became. The beings that walked around like ghosts were actually real people, real Alaskan Native people, and they were begging for money. Sometimes they had to prop themselves up next to doorways or windows because they were too drunk to stand on their own. I

felt for them and saw in them the waste of a beautiful culture, a culture that had taught their ancestors how to survive, and even thrive, in such a harsh environment that is Alaska. The Native people I saw seemed to have lost the spirit they once called upon for personal power.

They seemed to have lost their reason for living.

I learned later that it was customary for many of them to fly into Anchorage from some small nearby village, get drunk on the money the US government handed out to them as a living stipend, end up in a hospital in Anchorage, and when well enough to return to their village, get on an airplane to go back until the next month's government check arrived.

As for the Native women in town, most of the ones I saw practiced prostitution, and when I looked into their faces, their eyes were glazed over from drugs or alcohol consumption.

Back in Switzerland, when I read about Anchorage, I had conjured up romantic images of what I expected it to be like. Surely I'd find freshly scrubbed, lace-curtained, bed-and-breakfast inns, as well as raucous rustic saloons, horse hookups, and clean window storefronts filled with stacks of survival gear, all beckoning me to enter. In my mind both sides of town would be just like you'd see on a Hollywood set for a Western TV show.

But I discovered that Anchorage had an unimaginative heart, and only commerce coursed through its brown and dusty veins. Anchorage's economy is dominated by the fishing, natural gas, and oil industries, but it also hosted a fair number of people transporting and distributing living essentials from the lower forty-eight states and other countries. Most of Alaska's imports arrive by ship, and trucks deliver the goods to the rest of the state after fanning out from the port of Anchorage. There was scant evidence that Anchorage invested any revenue its businesses collected into any social or structural improvements.

One thing Anchorage did have that I was grateful for was a big sporting goods shop. Tobias and I visited it, wanting to purchase mountaineering skis. (Downhill skis bind the whole foot; the bindings on mountaineering skis are unattached at the back of the foot, which makes it easier to climb up a mountain in them.)

But we were out of luck. The shop carried only regular cross-country skies. Cross-country skis are constructed with the kind of bindings we needed, but they're also narrower and less sturdy than mountaineering skis. Nevertheless, we each bought a pair, and I silently hoped they would hold up well on any rugged Alaskan mountain.

The shop also sold Sorel boots, a type of boot that is made of rubber, and insulated on the inside. We figured they'd be very practical in the spring and fall if we needed to forge cold mountain streams, or accidently slipped into one.

And for winter we discovered "bunny boots," the Extreme Cold Vapor Barrier Boots used by the United States armed forces, which retain warmth by sandwiching up to one inch of wool and felt insulation between two layers of rubber. Because of this clever assembly of insulation materials, the boots are guaranteed to keep feet warm in outside temperatures up to minus sixty degrees Fahrenheit. Making this last purchase gave me great comfort as I considered the dead of winter to come.

Tobias and I also came across some information that almost changed the whole course of my plan.

A lady there told us about a nearby cabin she owned. The cabin was built on Lake Louise, about two hundred miles northeast of Anchorage.

"You might enjoy staying through the winter in my cabin," she offered, "if you want to."

Tobias turned an eye toward me, excited about the offer.

In just that one eye I could see hope.

Anchorage had dampened his spirits. Maybe we could pull back on our plan. Maybe this lady's cabin would compel me to relinquish my commitment to living a thousand miles or more away from any other living soul... Maybe continuing with that plan really was complete craziness?

Surely two hundred miles from civilization would be enough?

I hesitated only a moment before giving the lady an answer.

I didn't need to seriously ponder this generous offer. I knew the

deep end of the wilderness wasn't just two hundred miles away. I didn't want people ice-fishing near my winter home, or buzzing over Lake Louise on skidoos.

No, I decided. This cabin definitely wasn't removed enough from human activity for what I was seeking.

"Tobias and I are headed for the Interior," I explained to that kind lady.

And just a little, Tobias' shoulders slumped.

The challenge from the beginning was a *Weiterbildung*...to go further...

| **13** |

SEEKERS & DELIVERERS

The bi-level train from Anchorage to Fairbanks left the station at eight o'clock in the morning, chugging along its tracks at a soft twenty-five to thirty miles an hour. Tobias and I stood on the top level, sitting only intermittently. For the eight-hour length of the trip, Tobias stayed on the top of that train with me. He was like my shadow.

But Alaska stretched out ahead. One million five hundred thousand square kilometers of it. Twice the size of Texas and larger than the total area of the twenty-two smallest states in the lower forty-eight. "Five hundred eighty-six thousand square miles." That's what the woman in the shop said the size was, "in American."

I was counting on fishing in one of Alaska's three million lakes. Three million! I couldn't get my head around that number.

And I would come face to face with a glacier or two in the interior. That was for sure. Alaska was home to one hundred thousand of them --- equal to half of all the glaciers in the entire world.

Did the Russian Empire know what it was selling to the United States when it accepted 7.2 million U.S. dollars for all this land in 1867? I'm not a businessman, but four dollars and eighty cents per square kilometer (or less than two cents an acre "in American") sounds like a deal to me, even for a deal struck a hundred and fifty

years ago.

Russia was fresh out of money after fighting, and losing, the Crimean War --- a short but expensive disagreement with France, Britain and the Ottoman Empire --- fought to determine who would control Christian minorities in the Holy Land. Also fought, no doubt, over who would control the Holy Land itself. Russia wanted to, and France, Britain and the Ottoman Empire preferred Russia didn't.

As for the Alaskan Territory, Russia had never committed financial resources to support major settlements --- or even a military presence --- there. No more than four hundred settlers could ever be counted in the whole region. Russia also feared that if there was some future conflict with the British, the British could easily infiltrate into Alaskan Territory from British Columbia and steal away the land.

The irony for Russia is that while it sought land and power in the Middle East, it forfeited a great land and powerful natural resources in Alaska.

Did the United States know what treasure it had acquired?

William Seward, Secretary of State under Presidents Abraham Lincoln and Andrew Johnson, arranged the deal with Russia. Seward was a lawyer and a lifelong statesman who was enthusiastic about expanding the territory of the United States. After the end of America's Civil War in 1865, Seward worked passionately to develop new opportunities for trade and to establish a military presence wherever possible. Was Alaska too far west and too far north? He didn't think so.

Opponents of the purchase called it "Seward's Folly."

"What a waste," they complained. "Who would ever want to live in Seward's Icebox? It's just a garden for polar bears."

The critics had little thought for a person like me, a person seeking to find life answers and needing a wilderness to do it in.

The critics also had little thought for animal and mineral riches the land possessed.

But in 1897, surprising news reached William Seward's critics.

Two Alaska Natives and a man from Seattle found gold in some land up there near Alaska. Gold! Maybe this northwest region of the New World had something going for it after all.

Within a six-month period, over 100,000 prospectors (mostly through Seattle, Washington) set off for Dawson, a small settlement located in the Klondike region of the Yukon River territory, high up in the northwest corner of Canada, right east of the Alaskan border.

Planted in the breast of each prospector burned a make-it-rich-quick desire for gold.

When I read about these prospectors, I wondered: Did they go in prepared?

In life, whatever the quest, that's what I always looked for in others. That's what I always asked of myself.

Northwest Mounted Police in Canada tried to force a preparation system on the Klondikers. They demanded that all gold-seekers bring a year's worth of supplies with them from Alaska into Canada. How they checked, I can't be sure, since there were two trails prospectors could use to reach Dawson.

One of the trails --- the White Pass Trail --- originated in Skagway, Alaska. The town would boom, and America would see that Alaska was not a wasteland.

But Skagway eventually garnered bad press because of a con-man named Jefferson "Soapy" Smith. Soapy and three hundred of his men conducted scamming operations in town and along the trail. One scam involved constructing telegraph poles and wires along White Pass --- wires and poles that resembled a communication system but weren't actually connected to anything! Soapy conned cash from Klondikers impatient to wire messages home.

You had to look out on the White Pass Trail for lurking men who were determined to deceive and steal.

You had to be prepared for that. Still, White Pass' narrow and slippery route was overcrowded. Pack horses traveled with the prospectors and many of the exhausted animals got bogged down in mud and toppled over the cliffs. Or they starved to death. Jack London, the writer, called White Pass the "Dead Horse Trail."

If prospectors decided they didn't want to be conned, and preferred fewer outlaws along their journey, they could choose the Chilkoot Trail that originated in Dyea, Alaska. It was even steeper than the White Pass Trail. Old historical pictures show men climbing up the first steep path out of Dyea in single file. What city man could have been fully prepared for the tough terrain that awaited him beyond the first ridge? How could he maneuver "a year's worth" of cumbersome supplies over steep and unpredictable pathways?

Many of the prospectors on both trails turned back, lost their way, or died from the cold. Malnutrition and starvation were serious threats, too. I read of one Klondiker who boiled his boots so he could drink the broth. Only 30,000 of the original 100,000 reached their goal. And most of those who succeeded in reaching Dawson left empty-handed. And yet, when news reached Dawson that other men were finding gold in Nome, Alaska, the Klondikers who had been unsuccessful in the Yukon Territory clambered to get to Nome.

When a determined person has a goal, it's hard to stop him or her until the goal is realized.

And now here I was, not on a trail but a train, clambering to reach my goal.

My "instrument" responded melodiously to Fairbanks right away. It was a compact, friendly town. The permanent residents offered welcoming smiles, and there were few tourists like me roaming the streets. Lucky for that because --- as in Anchorage --- no sidewalks existed in Fairbanks except for the immediate downtown area. The houses were smaller than in Anchorage and there were fewer commercial structures, although the campus of the University of Alaska, if you consider that a place of commerce, was quite big. The university was and probably still is Fairbanks' largest employer. At that time, most of the students at UAF were Americans from the lower forty-eighty states, but quite a big percentage of Alaska Natives also attended.

Most newcomers to Fairbanks had come for the thrill --- the thrill of earning quick money --- quicker money than they could come by in any other city across the US. Working for an oil

company assured you of earning liquid gold, and plenty of it.

And there were other attractions as well.

Residents of Alaska paid neither a sales tax nor a state income tax. And if, as an American citizen, you managed to live (survive) in the climate for more than one year, you would receive, free of tax, an annual payment of more than one thousand dollars, because of a "thank you for letting us use your land" fund set up by the oil businesses. It seemed an attractive life. An easy life, even.

Yet I heard often of the results of those who had failed to realize that in any part of Alaska, a person has to be prepared. Soapy Smith may be long gone, but the terrain, animals and treacherous weather remain. Just because "civilization" is somewhere nearby does not mean you can ignore certain rules for survival.

For instance, in the winter, when the temperatures go down to forty or fifty below zero, it can be very dangerous to be caught outdoors, even in what you think will be a warm car or truck. You have to constantly make sure your vehicle is running well, and be prepared if it breaks down or if you get lost in the middle of a whiteout. During a whiteout, wind-blown snow can accelerate up to forty miles per hour, and severely reduce your visibility. There are no reference points and your orientation will be badly distorted. People can get lost in their own backyards, even if the door to their house is only ten feet away. If you're driving, you've got to stop your car, because it's impossible to see. You must have survival supplies and blankets with you at all times.

A group of guys Tobias and I met were still mourning two friends who had died in a whiteout the winter before. The two friends had been in Fairbanks for just a few months, and had failed to prepare. Upon hearing any news such as this, Tobias would raise his eyebrows at me with the question: Have we prepared enough?

In Zurich I played volleyball in a club with Rebecca, an older woman with perpetually sad eyes but a kind voice. When she learned of my upcoming trip to Alaska, she confided that her only daughter had escaped to Fairbanks two years before. Rebecca asked me to return a repaired watch to her daughter. I agreed to do so. The difficulty was that the only contact information Rebecca possessed for her daughter, Fabienne, was a Post Office

box number.

Before the Klondike and Nome gold rushes in the late 1800s and early 1900s, there was scant need for mail service. Most of the indigenous Alaskan people were illiterate. But the new prospectors weren't. They brought with them the habit of writing letters, and demanded regular mail service as a way to connect to their family, friends and business partners back home. If they managed to get around Soapy Smith, they still wanted to send and receive letters.

Mail carriers used dogsleds to deliver the mail back then, sloshing up snowy peaks and through unpredictable woodlands. Because of their dedication to making sure all letters got delivered to their correct destinations, high winds and easily spooked wildlife didn't stop them. Even when the trails between mail cabins and roadhouses were lost in the snow, they persevered. If conditions were good and mail loads were light, a carrier could travel between twenty to thirty miles in a day.

Tobias and I had come over three thousand miles to deliver one package. We were the modern-day mail carriers who traveled by airplane, just like modern-day mail carriers in Alaska.

In Fairbanks, then, at the Post Office, I left a note, stating that I was looking for Fabienne, that I had something to give her from her mother, and that I would be pitching a tent at the Tanana River camp, about a forty-five minute walk outside of town.

The next Saturday morning, Fabienne and her husband, Peter, came knocking on my tent's front door. A blond-haired girl of about two years old stood between them, rocking back and forth on her feet and holding her hands behind her. Her name was Petra, and she reminded me of Reguli.

After some time Fabienne and Peter offered up these details of their lives: that Fabienne had failed to find work as a nurse in Fairbanks, and was currently unemployed; that Peter drove a school bus for the Fairbanks school system during the scholastic year, and that he also, during the summer months, was unemployed.

Fabienne and Peter had settled in a hut at Goldstream Valley, about ten miles north of Fairbanks.

Being a little homesick, Fabienne and Peter were happy to have

fellow countrymen around, and it was comforting for us to meet and get to know people from Switzerland who knew Alaska. So it wasn't long before we were invited to move our tents to their backyard, and we accepted the invitation to stay through the summer months. Their hut was one of five or six clustered together on a flat piece of landscape, and because they appeared to have just popped out of the ground, everybody knew these houses as The Mushrooms.

While camped out in the backyard, Tobias and I helped buy food, prepare food, and (since there was no running water inside the Mushroom) carry water for cooking and washing the dishes. Luckily we were able to take hot showers at the University of Alaska in Fairbanks. Lots of people like us willingly paid a quarter for this privilege.

Now that we have our bearings, I thought with anticipation, we can plan our first canoe trip.

But we soon found out that we couldn't plan any canoe trips until the river breakup.

River breakup?

This was a new concept for me. We have frozen rivers in Switzerland, but if ice melts, it melts away. Never like it does in Alaska, and never this late in the season. The guidebooks didn't prepare me for this.

Yukon river ice can be five or six feet thick in winter. Cars even drive on Alaskan rivers in winter, which means that it would take an awful lot of heat to melt river ice. The river breakup happens not because sun melts the river ice. The sun does melt some of the ice in the river, but not much. The sun will melt the snow on top of the ice, as well as the snow on the shores of the river. It is because there is an extraordinary amount of melting going on around the river that the water level of the river starts to rise. Because of all the water filling up the river channels, the water is able to lift up the ice that sat all winter in the channels. What is lifted up then starts to float. Solid chunks will crack as they begin to move. Then there might be a slab that will be caught along the river's edge, and another piece bumps into it. The slab will crack and separate and bump into other pieces of ice as the current

moves underneath them all. Some chunks will be pushed ashore. Others will continue on their way, being bumped or broken or cracked by other pieces that push their way through the maze of chunks. When river ice cracks and bumps there are tremendous popping, hissing, crunching, grating and grinding noises. The river becomes a percussion orchestra. It becomes a freight train crashing along the riverbank. It becomes an ice tray from a giant's freezer, cracking apart when the giant decides to fix himself a large, cold Coca-Cola.

Tobias and I rode the ice chunks on the Tanana River that spring, fascinated by their strength, beauty, and amazing oddness compared to anything else we had ever seen or known.

While we waited for the rivers to return to a more liquid state, Peter mentioned that he had been hired to build a log cabin further into the woods and asked if we wanted to see it. Looking for something to do, Tobias and I offered to help with the construction. I wasn't just thinking about helping Peter and Fabienne, but also about the possibility of learning something for myself. Maybe I could learn enough to build a log cabin when I returned to Switzerland?

Tobias and I received our initial construction education by finishing the cabin's walls. Step one was to peel felled logs of their outer bark...and the work became much more detailed from that initial simple first step.

With the aid of a few how-to-construct-a-cabin books bought in town, I applied myself diligently to finishing the two-room, two-story house, with electricity, as soon as possible.

But Peter was a peculiar sort of human being. He did things much differently than I would have done them. He was never in a hurry. For instance, if we needed a nail, Peter would drive an hour and a half into town to buy one nail, and then drive back again. "Peter, why not buy a whole box of nails?" I would ask, and in response he would only smile at me.

I wasn't in a position to judge that kind of behavior. One of the few positive things about the Swiss Army is that it forces a person to adjust to others who are different from you. In the army you can't get away from the other fellow. You have to find a way

to understand in order to deflect the annoying irritations that are sure to come when you are huddled together with a group of one hundred fellows for eighteen weeks with no chance of escape. Sleeping next to a guy who doesn't brush his teeth for a week because it saves time in the morning made me think that if I had grown up in the same type of circumstances as he had, then I might be doing the same crazy things he did.

In watching Peter, I was struck by the fact that even though he had very little money to live on and at the present didn't have a roof of his own over his head, I never saw him complain about his circumstances.

Fabienne did, though. She longed to go back to Switzerland. She was upset that Peter refused to look for a real job that could feed and house a family. Fabienne wasn't just preoccupied with the two-year-old little girl who dawdled at her feet. Another child was on the way.

The truth is, I wanted to be more like Peter in certain ways. I wanted to be able to slow down, to step back, and to look at things from a different point of view. Wasn't that one of the reasons I was here in Alaska?

Tobias formed his own relationship with Peter and Fabienne. Up until that point, he had never changed a diaper, taken care of a feverish child, or dealt with a crying baby. Funny to me that being in Alaska was forcing Tobias into becoming a family man. And he learned quickly. Yet his ability to express himself verbally remained clumsy and discomfited. But he tried. He took baby steps.

| 14 |

THE ESKIMO

Visitors to Alaska often want to become familiar with all six of its geographic regions, but my plan was to occupy myself in only one, or possibly two, of them: the Interior region and the Arctic region.

The Interior region includes land in the central part of the state, between the Alaska Mountain Range to the south and the Brooks Mountain Range to the north.

The Arctic region is the area that lies along the northern border of Alaska, from the edge of the Brooks Mountain Range all the way to the Arctic Ocean.

I would leave the Southwest, South Central, Southeast, and Western territories for another time.

What type of Native inhabitants could I expect to encounter meandering in and around Fairbanks, the Interior's largest city? And what type of people would I find if I traveled somewhere near the Arctic?

Five major indigenous groups co-existed in Alaska when Russian explorers discovered it in 1741.

The Aleuts were the first of the indigenous groups the Russians stumbled upon. The Aleuts lived then (and still do) in the Aleutian Islands, that long broken necklace of landmasses floating between Russia and Alaska. The Russians were happy to trade their trinkets for the furs of Aleutian beaver, otter, seal, and fox. And the Aleuts

were happy to share their language with the Russians to help them name the land. The Aleut word for Alaska is *Alaxsxaq*, which means *the object toward which the action of the sea is directed*.

How fitting that the place which had called and drawn me to an inward journey was named after a word that signifies *magnet*. Alaxsxaq was the object toward which the action of my person was being directed.

But I would not be visiting the Aleutian Islands.

If the Russians had traveled further east, they would have encountered the Southeast Coastal Indians (a second major indigenous group which includes the Tlingit, Haida, Eyak, and Tsimshian tribes) who live close to the Canadian and US borders. All four of these groups are neighbors, but they spoke (and speak) different languages and operate separate social systems.

But I would not be visiting the Southeast Coast of Alaska.

I would, however, be traipsing through the Interior region of the state where Athabascans, also called Interior Indians, make their home. History says that Athabascans liked to set up camp along the rivers, so I looked forward to meeting some of them on the Yukon, the Tanana, the Susita, the Kuskokwim --- or whichever river Tobias and I canoed. But if we came upon them as they fished, hunted and trapped for their survival, would they assume we were interfering with their resources, or would they accept us and be willing to share? And if they were not hunting, nor fishing nor trapping, would they be happily settled in cozy villages along the rivers, with their old nomadic way of life long put aside? Those were things we would have to learn.

And even though I didn't plan to loiter along the Arctic's North Shore, I hoped that I might get close enough to meet a Yupik or Inupiaq Eskimo, a member of one of Alaska's two indigenous groups who live there.

Don't fault me for using the term *Eskimo*. All aboriginal inhabitants of the Arctic region, which extends from Russia through Alaska, Canada and into Greenland, used to answer to this name. Only recently have the Inuit peoples in Canada decided that *Eskimo* is a derogatory term, and now prefer to be called *Inuit*.

But the Yupik and Inupiaq, the final two of the five indigenous groups in Alaska, are still called Eskimos.

Aboriginal inhabitants of the Arctic and Sub-Arctic regions of the earth can be divided into three groups: The Inuit, Yupik, and Inupiaq. Each group claims a unique cultural heritage, a unique language, and a general geographic location.

All Inuit, Yupik and Inupiaq peoples are *Eskimo*, which means either *eater of raw meat* or *he laces snowshoes*, depending on which language you use to mine the word's origin.

The Eskimos of Canada are Inuit.

The Eskimos of Alaska are Yupik and Inupiaq.

Yupik (meaning real people) are Eskimos, but they are neither Inuit nor Inupiaq. At first the Yupik Alaska Natives lived on the tundra-covered lowlands, which provided many opportunities for fishing, foraging, and hunting. But slowly the Yupik advanced southward, up the rivers where they encountered Athabascans, with whom they shared the land, water, mountains and sky. Now Yupik peoples are known to live south of the Seward Peninsula along the Bering Sea coast and in the deltas of the Yukon and Kuskokwim rivers. Some say the Yupik in Alaska might even be able to speak with their "relatives" in Russia, since Yupik peoples live in Russia as well as Alaska and all Yupik share common language roots.

According to history, the Yupik Eskimos hunted sea mammals but relied on salmon for the major portion of their food.

Along the rivers, then, I expected that Tobias and I would meet both Athabascans (meat eaters) and Yupik Eskimos (salmon eaters). Contrast and compare: better to eat moose? Or salmon?

The Inupiaq Natives of Alaska are a sub-group of the Inuit in Canada, but distinct from it because of variances in their two language systems.

Inupiaq Eskimos have occupied the northern shores of Alaska for perhaps four thousand years.

They are the ones who, along with the Yupik, hunt whale and

eat blubber and live in igloos, or so my grammar school geography book said. To survive the harsh Arctic environment, they developed a profound understanding of the area's land, animals, sea, and weather, as well as the skill to exploit all of the area's available resources. All of these things captured my imagination, and I longed to follow the tracks of people who understood these things. I was eager to meet a "real" Eskimo, and learn from him.

For this reason whenever I walked anywhere in Fairbanks or its surrounding areas, I did so with great anticipation. Fairbanks was situated fairly close to the Arctic region, and in the areas where we lived and worked I thought I'd easily come across an Arctic Yupik or Inupiaq Eskimo.

But I was wrong.

Weeks passed without my seeing any Native at all.

So when I found myself next to one the first time I stopped for coffee at Jamie's Health Shop in downtown Fairbanks, I could hardly contain my excitement.

With great curiosity I stared as he stood patiently beside me at the coffee bar, waiting to place his order. This Eskimo couldn't have been taller than about five feet and four inches, and was dressed in trousers, a work shirt and a well-worn animal jacket. When he saw that I was stealing glances at him, he turned his attention fully toward me. His eyes belied his gray-white hair and creased face. They were young eyes, and glimmered like diamonds.

"Your name is --- what?" the Eskimo asked as he extended a wide, brown hand with short fingers.

I smiled, caught. "Ruedi," I answered, and grasped his calloused palm.

"From where --- are you?" he asked next.

When I answered that I was from Switzerland, his brow knotted and he looked away.

"It's a very tiny country in Europe," I told him. "Where are you from?"

The Eskimo said he was from the north shore of Alaska, and in town now to visit one of his relatives.

"Just...just wondering," I stammered as I searched his round face to see if he might be offended, "do you live in an igloo there?"

Now the Eskimo smiled, and there was joy in his eyes.

"In Europe everybody thinks Eskimos still live in igloos," I quickly added in an attempt to hide my ignorance.

My new acquaintance motioned for me to join him at a table by the window where he sat down. In the process of seating myself, I watched him lift his coffee cup to his nose and hold it there as he breathed in the coffee's aroma. I smiled. That's exactly what I do before I take a first sip of coffee. The Eskimo smiled back and shrugged. "The way it smells --- I enjoy very much," he said.

He did not take a drink immediately, but instead placed his cup neatly on the table. I studied the creases on the backs of his leathered hands and fingers.

"About the igloos ---," he began, reminding me of the question I had asked and felt I should have known the answer to but didn't, "we stay in them --- but not all the time. Just during hunting season. We use a snow saw to carve blocks of hard packed snow out of the ground. The blocks are about two or three feet long and about a foot high and almost a foot deep. We place the blocks in a circle, trimming the sides slightly at the tops so the blocks rest inward together. Then more smaller blocks are stacked on top of the first circle of blocks until the circle, getting smaller and smaller, is closed at the top. Two men can build one igloo in less than an hour."

"When I was young it took me longer than that to set up a tent," I said.

He laughed softly. "In the past during the winter we Eskimos lived in the ground. To give structure to our houses and to prevent the surrounding sod from caving in we used whale skeletons. Big spaces --- they were not --- but they were functional." He paused and bent his head down to blow on the hot coffee. He still hadn't taken a sip of it. Then he looked up and said, "Living in the ground can keep a person very warm --- you know?" He turned his head and looked at me sideways as if I might not believe him.

But I nodded. That made sense to me because in Switzerland

when I would hike in the mountains in winter I would often dig a cavity from a mound of snow, position my sleeping bag in it, and have a night of warm rest inside. Living under the earth might be much warmer than living above it, indeed.

"Electricity --- we did not have then," the Eskimo continued. "Instead --- we used small oil lamps for lighting and for heating --- and a small amount of oil could keep us warm. We harvested oil from whales by boiling their blubber. In the ground we lived and above ground we buried our dead. Ground in winter is much too hard to dig through. So a pyre of stones on top of the body --- we would build --- to bury a person. In that way wild animals could not violate the body."

Finally the Eskimo picked up his coffee and took a small sip. "But white people came along and told us 'Live above the ground --- you must,' and 'Bury your people below --- you must.'" He paused and searched my face, shaking his head. "Do you know what?" he asked.

I shook my head.

"Since we have changed --- since doing what they say --- since then --- most everyone is cold."

"Well, then why did you change?" I asked.

The Eskimo looked intently into my eyes. "What I now understand requires more words than I am used to speaking. Do you have time to listen?"

I had barely looked at my watch since arriving in Alaska. There were no appointments for new work, and no deadlines to complete old work. Yes, I had time.

The Eskimo took another small sip of his coffee. "In harmony with nature we lived. A people in harmony with nature once we were. I talk about people in my parents' time --- when I was a very young boy. We didn't live in big cities because we could never find in one place the things we needed to survive. To feed our families we hunted, fished, and scavenged for roots and berries. Providing enough food required us to constantly move about. But happy --- we were. I think this was so because --- we understood something many people today do not --- accept?" He had looked over my

shoulder to search for the word *accept*.

"Life is more than physical things. It is more than what we see with our eyes. You understand?" He paused, and with a lowered voice asked, "Feel the energy that comes from the earth --- do you?"

I couldn't believe what I was hearing. "I do," I answered.

"Well, this energy --- this energy that with our eyes --- we cannot see --- this energy that with our being --- we can sense --- we can feel --- this energy is what we called *spirit*. My ancestors taught that this energy is just as important as the physical world --- maybe more --- even?"

I nodded. My father was the only other person whom I had ever heard put this idea into words.

"Both are important. My people believed --- and certain they were --- that the physical world --- in harmony with the spiritual world --- should co-exist. It was not good --- it was not healthy --- it could be dangerous --- for either world to ignore the other."

As the Eskimo hesitantly searched for words, my thoughts drifted to the long-ago times I spent with my father skiing or hiking. He emphasized how important it was to pay attention to not just what we saw. We had to pay attention to what we felt on the glaciers or in the mountains. If we ignored the information our heightened senses received, it could have been dangerous, or even fatal, for us.

Now this Eskimo was talking about how energy wasn't just in the mountains or on the glacier, but everywhere.

"Our communities developed men and women to become skilled in dealing with the spiritual world. Shamans we called them." When he said the word, the Eskimo sounded almost like he was singing. The Eskimo's whole way of speaking changed the cadence of the English I knew. No word nor syllable was emphasized where I expected it. But rather than find it disturbing, I was drawn by it. Listening to his voice was like listening to music.

"Wise men and wise women --- we knew them to be. The shamans helped us to remain in harmony with each other and with the earth --- with the energy that we could not see."

"They were your priests, then?" I asked.

"Exactly --- not," the Eskimo answered. "They played different roles." He spread his hands and wiggled his fingers, saying, "They had to have more than one skill. Teachers --- they were. They taught us how to treat one another and how to care for the earth. Judges --- too --- they were --- when our behavior --- needed correction. And rememberers of our traditions --- they were. Often --- I remember --- how my mother and my father repeated shaman stories of old."

"They sound like very wise people," I interjected.

"Exactly --- they were. A shaman was also a physician. In the time of my parents the shamans were quite familiar with the human body. Maybe a shaman at that time knew just as much as any Western doctor?"

I shook my head and shrugged. This was all new information to me.

The Eskimo went on. "One thing you must know about illness --- and what it was my people believed. You will think it strange --- perhaps?"

I lifted my shoulders to shrug once more. "I don't..." I was going to say, "I don't think anything yet," but he continued without my having to say.

"If a person becomes injured --- he may suffer pain. If a person takes in a poison --- he may become sick. The shamans knew how to deal with both types of ailments. They identified where to find a wide variety of herbs and plants that could minimize the effect of an injury, and they practiced preparing animal remedies to combat a poison or to aid in recovery.

"But other types of illnesses --- there also were. My people believed other illnesses could come because an evil spirit invaded the body. How to rid the body of an evil spirit? The shamans figured they had to access different powers. No herbs nor tinctures nor animal parts could be used to fight an evil-spirit illness. This type needed more. Chants and drums and dancing were needed to convince an evil spirit to depart the afflicted person. The shamans --- and we --- for many, many years used chants and drums and

dancing to treat evil-spirit diseases. Our tradition --- it was. Our way --- it remained --- for many, many years."

After upending our table's peppershaker the Eskimo sprinkled some of its contents on the white formica tabletop. "Our villages were scattered like these pepper bits," he said. "But most of the native people here in Alaska shared common beliefs. One of the things we believed was --- that people were always more important than things." He shook his head. "Our lives were not about accumulating things."

The Eskimo picked up a flint coffee stirrer from the table and held the ends between his two middle fingers. "Every few years we could make new tools when our tools from animal-bones became less sharp. When animal skins wore out, we could sew new coverings with fresh animal skins. We could leave our tools and clothes to disintegrate outside if we no longer needed them."

He put the stirrer down by the saltshaker. "Our lives --- were not about accumulating things," he repeated.

Holding out the thumb of his left hand, he began to enumerate the distinct beliefs and practices of his people. "Hoard --- we did not."

Up went the index finger when he said, "Waste --- we did not."

Indicating the middle finger, "Back to the earth --- we gave --- what it --- to us --- had given."

And pulling on the ring finger he continued, "Our traditions taught us to care for those who did not have and who were in need. If someone traveling in the wilderness appeared --- what heat and shelter and food we had --- we shared. That --- was our custom."

He held his fingers in front of me. "Our shared traditions --- these were."

Though I was certainly pretty ignorant of Biblical scriptures, this idea of caring reminded me of when I was a child and the stories I had heard of how the early Christians shared all they had to provide for each one's needs. It seemed like a beautiful thing.

The Eskimo began to "walk" the fingers of his left hand across

the table. "When --- a long time ago --- Westerners wandered onto our land," his fingers paused next to my hand that rested near my coffee cup, "they saw a people different from them. Our faces --- our eyebrows and lips --- were punctured with wooden studs or animal-bones to communicate strength and beauty. To keep our skin from cracking in this dry climate we used seal oil, which is very smelly. We couldn't wash frequently or take many baths. The White men held their noses --- often." He smiled slightly and shrugged. "In underground houses framed in by whalebones --- we lived --- and things can get smelly there.

"The way we dressed --- the way we smelled --- the way we lived --- the way we danced --- all these ways were offensive to the Westerners who --- for furs and gold --- came to hunt. They did not understand our methods for curing disease. They could not comprehend how dancing and chanting and drumming could rid a community of illness. Frightened --- were they?" He looked at me and smiled. "We believed that we were giving help to the Westerners when we shared with them our homes and food, as well as the knowledge of our spiritual world. We wanted to help them understand how important it was to pay attention to the spirit. But what we did not know --- could not know --- until too late --- was that Westerners did not want to understand our ways."

The Eskimo shook his head, and for the first time looked sad.

I can't explain it, but seeing him this way made me sad. I had opened myself up to understand him, and he played his bow on my heart strings.

The Eskimo paused, and remained silent. His coffee was growing cold. Finally he remembered it and took a small sip. "The White Man brought some good things," he repeated, "but he also brought with him some very bad things. Do you know what the most harmful thing he brought --- was?"

I thought for a moment and then answered unsurely, like a novice at the feet of his master, "His gun?"

He smiled at me kindly and said, "His gun has been destructive to our land, it is true --- but what he brought that was most harmful was --- his way of seeing."

"His way of seeing?" I asked. I didn't understand

"The way he saw us worked to destroy us. It was his attitude. When the White Man saw how we lived and dressed and healed ourselves, the White man judged us --- he did. He looked at us and thought --- perhaps --- that we were not human beings?" There was a question in his voice. He raised his eyebrows and looked away for a long moment. When he turned back to me he said, "This one thing --- this judgment --- worked silently. This judgment destroyed our confidence in who we were as a people." The Eskimo shook his head. He had spoken simply, and there was no harshness to his voice at all.

"I'm sorry," I said, because I didn't know what else to say. I really was sorry.

"Something to add --- I must. To suffer his judgment --- to survive his presence in our world --- we might have been able to do --- if not for something else."

My body tensed, remembering the ghostlike creatures I saw in Anchorage. "It was the alcohol, then, wasn't it?"

"No," he said gently. "No. Of course the alcohol is now a curse --- true that is. My people now drink too much of it. But no. No. What swarmed in with the Westerners were diseases we had never known before."

Mr. Eskimo remained silent for a very long moment.

"Many, many people died. Too many. Parents. Children. Uncles. Cousins. Whole villages --- sometimes. Orphans --- many became. An orphan I became. Twelve years old --- I was then."

These words plucked a sharp chord within me. I was twelve when my father died, and although I was not left an orphan because my mother still lived, it was as though I had been. From the time my father died until that moment when I sat in the coffee shop, my mother rarely spoke to me. When she did I heard her tiny voice as if it came from a minuscule seed inside a cavernous shell. I had grown up an orphan.

The Eskimo spoke again, striking different strings on my instrument.

"It happened --- when they came for gold. The deaths --- I mean. The time I remember --- when the Westerners came --- is the time they now call the great Gold Rush. One of the worst times --- that was. The time of the Great Death --- that was.

"We did not know the diseases the Westerners brought with them. The remedies for them --- we did not have --- and recover --- we could not. The shamans were ignorant of things like small pox --- measles --- influenza. They didn't have remedies for them. Dancing --- chanting --- drumming --- could not cure them. I have heard that during that time --- more than half of all Alaska Natives --- were no more. And you know --- with so many deaths --- the spirit of our people --- died too --- I think."

"What happened to the shamans, then?" I asked.

The Eskimo tapped a thick forefinger on the table. "The trust my parents and grandparents had placed in the shamans --- greatly weakened. The shamans had failed. If they could not cure --- perhaps everything they taught and spoke about was false? How could my grandparents or parents call on them anymore? And if the shamans had failed --- in whom could my ancestors --- in what could my parents --- believe? The shamans had connected my people to the spiritual world --- and without the shamans --- my people stopped paying attention to the spiritual part of their lives."

The Eskimo sat straight up as if he were listening to a voice from an unseen source.

"When the missionaries appeared and taught us about their God, they assumed everything we knew about the spiritual world was of no use. The White explorers and fur traders and gold rushers complained that Natives here in Alaska were going about life the wrong way. They judged a whole culture --- to be wrong." He paused and studied his hands. "Our whole culture --- was not wrong. Many good things we had. And have."

The Eskimo's piercing eyes drilled into me once more. I looked away. The Eskimo was quiet.

When he spoke again, he did so very softly.

"Even so, it was the missionaries that the White men brought

with them who offered some very important knowledge to our people --- ideas we had only partly understood."

I was intrigued. Whatever missionaries would have taught the Eskimos I had ignored since childhood. "What was...important?" I asked hesitantly.

"At the time of the shamans it was our custom to give reverence to both Good and Evil --- Light and Dark --- all the negative and positive forces at work all around us. We worshipped each one --- believing that each force was equal."

"I believe so, too," I admitted, more to myself than to the Eskimo.

"Well --- when the missionaries came and lived among us --- they hurried to teach us about the Ruler of all that is negative and evil in the world. 'This Ruler is an invisible force' --- they said. We rolled our eyes because --- this --- of course --- we knew.

"But then they gave this force a name. Ruler of the Air --- they called it --- a weaker force and not to be trusted."

The Eskimo paused. "Now this surprised us."

It surprised me, too. My Army-Radio days had taught that negative and positive forces were equally at work, and why trust one above another?

"He wasn't to be trusted because of another name he has --- Father of Lies."

"What could a *force* lie about?" I asked. It wasn't quite making sense.

"Well --- the missionaries explained that this force is --- a personality. They said he is called the Father of Lies because he whispers to human beings that the earth has no beginning and will have no end."

The Eskimo paused again, waited for me to absorb this, and then continued.

"The missionaries also called him --- Prince of Darkness --- because he is always working to destroy light."

"But...light always destroys darkness!" I exclaimed, being totally absorbed in the story. "That's just the way a candle works in a dark

room. Even a tiny flame can make a whole room bright."

The Eskimo smiled. "Yes, you are right. But the missionaries taught us to think about light in various ways. 'Knowledge brings light to the mind' --- they said --- 'and truth brings light to the soul' --- they said." He paused, trying to discern if I understood, and saw the question on my face.

"Do you want to know how the Prince of Darkness destroys light?" he asked me.

Of course I was curious.

"The missionaries said the Prince of Darkness destroys light by making people question what is true --- about themselves --- and about the creator of the world. He distorts and confuses information about where human beings have come from in the beginning --- and where they are going in the end. Not knowing these truths would keep a person in a kind of darkness --- don't you think?"

I nodded slowly and wondered ever so faintly --- purely because the Eskimo seemed convinced of all that he spoke --- if my mind or soul had ever been influenced by this particular unseen force.

The Eskimo's whisper reached into my reverie. "And do you know what else the Prince of Darkness works very hard at? At preventing people from even enjoying light --- from recognizing that light is good --- that it creates everything --- that in it even love exists."

It was then that *my* brow furrowed, but before I could ask what light had to do with love, the Eskimo continued.

"When the missionaries gave us the final name for the ruler of earth's negative force --- calling him the Prince of Death --- we Alaska Natives trembled. Death was something we could not control --- death was something we could not appease. The missionaries said the Prince of Death is a powerful personality whose ultimate purpose is to kill and destroy. He prowls around like a ferocious wolverine --- seeking human beings to devour with his lies and deception. This Ruler of the Air --- Father of Lies --- Prince of Darkness --- Prince of Death --- holds death in his hands --- because no life blossoms with lies --- nor in darkness."

Hearing these words made me tremble, too, and I remained quiet.

"We Alaska Natives had never known the full extent of this negative force's personality --- but we had acknowledged that this force --- this he --- was powerful --- and we reasoned that it would be prudent to worship him so that his anger would be kept in check.

"And again the missionaries insisted --- 'No' --- saying that there is a force much greater than the Prince of Darkness. This force is the Light of the World --- a person --- too. 'He is the one you should worship' --- they said --- 'because it is through him that everything has been created. He also deserves worship because the Father of Heavenly Lights --- his father --- sent him to earth --- to do battle with the Prince of Darkness.'

"And then they explained --- that this is why there is distress in the world. There is a battle going on all around us."

Pictures of the veterans I had seen shuffling along the walkways of Anchorage and Fairbanks, TV images of the Vietnam War, and memories of my own visits to the Berlin Wall that continued to wrap a prison around East Berlin (and the rest of the Wall around all of East Germany) flashed across the screen of my mind. I couldn't disagree.

"But do you know what the missionaries insisted?" the Eskimo asked incredulously. "They insisted that the battle has already been won. 'The Light of the World has won' --- they said. 'The Prince of Darkness has been defeated.' They shared a story about the battle in which the Light of the World was killed because he didn't want the human beings he created to live in darkness. In the story, the Light of the World came back to life. It is a marvelous story and many of us believed it. Each time the missionaries told it they would add --- 'Now you don't have to live in darkness anymore.'"

He paused and smiled slightly. "'But still ---' we asked the missionaries --- 'If the Prince of Darkness has been defeated --- then why do storms --- disasters --- and even darkness and death --- continue to occur? It seems very clear that the Ruler of the Air still has great power.'"

His question seemed reasonable and I, too, wanted to know how the missionaries answered it.

"They explained that the Light of the World --- has not yet brought his enemy under his feet. 'That will only happen at the End' --- they said."

"At the End," I repeated.

"I did not understand this," the Eskimo said. Then he laid his hands on the table and squared his body to mine. "So I ask you --- Mr. Ruedi --- why does darkness continue and why does the End not come if the battle is already won?"

He searched my face as if I might really have the answer. Again, I remained quiet because up until then I was unfamiliar with the Light of whom the Eskimo spoke, and there were many things that the Eskimo said that I would have to sort out later.

"Don't worry if you don't know. This was a mystery the missionaries could not explain either. And I'm sorry for this because I really would like to know."

The Eskimo paused and held both hands over the left side of his chest.

"But one thing they assured us is this," he said, "that if we are willing to trust this Light of the World --- then the Prince of Death will have no power over us. I believe this and have come to know in my heart that this is true. So I am thankful for these good things the missionaries taught us."

Then the Eskimo clapped his hands and said with conviction, "But we had things to teach the White Man, too! The activity of the Prince of Darkness in the air --- still trying to deceive the human beings below --- can be felt in the negative vibrations flowing through the earth. Neither the fur trappers nor the gold rushers could prepare for these vibrations --- and neither the explorers nor the missionaries had enough experience to explain them.

"Alaska Natives possessed many years of knowledge that told us how to detect these vibrations in our environment and how to use them for survival. We know that everything is not bacteria and viruses. It is still important to recognize --- to identify --- the energy --- the electricity --- that runs through our environment.

There are positives and negatives to everything.

"The missionaries taught us about the one God who rules over all creation. But we could have taught them --- and those who brought them --- about the energy that invades our environment. Everything is energy. There is a positive and negative force behind everything we see and experience.

"We needed to learn about the God who came to rescue us from eternal death, but the White men and their missionaries needed to learn from us how to read the environment --- how to survive in a place so harsh and barren. We understood these things. The energy that courses through this earth is something with which human beings still must contend --- and we knew how.

"And we could have helped the missionaries teach their explorers and trappers and men hungry for gold about how to live peacefully with their neighbors. We knew how to do that --- too. We had lived in harmony with each other and with nature for centuries. Our souls may not have been pure --- but we had our customs which were important to keep a community functioning and at peace. We could have taught them those things.

"To me it is very sad that my people came to accept that they had nothing to teach."

The Eskimo drained the last sips of his coffee by turning his cup almost upside done. When he placed the cup back on the table he reminded me of my question.

"You asked me why my people --- changed their way of living." He shrugged his shoulders slightly. "We thought we had to change. We thought Westerners had more knowledge than we did. They came with mighty guns and mysterious technology. They seemed powerful and we treated them as our elders. 'To be healthy you must live in houses above ground' --- they said. 'To heat those new houses --- you must buy more fuel.'" A soft chuckle came from his throat, and he looked away as if remembering something. "But now --- if we run out of fuel --- which we do --- often --- because a lot of fuel is required to heat a house above ground in winter --- if we run out of fuel --- we get cold." He shook his head and let out a faint sigh.

He sat calmly in front of me. Had you seen him there, you would have read kindness in his face, and in his being a life seemingly untouched by trouble. I was amazed at his friendliness, his softness, and his generosity in sharing his thoughts.

"Thinking about all of this...doesn't it make you angry...at people...at people like...me? Or does it make you angry at...God?" I asked.

"Well," he answered, "Well. Decided --- I did --- accepted --- I did --- that there must be a reason --- for what has happened to us --- to me. These things --- were meant to be as they are. I trust --- that it is so."

His words took my breath away. How could someone whose history was full of adversity and heartache just accept it all? How could someone whose father and mother had been taken away from him at the age of twelve be able to trust that it was meant to be?

"Forgiven them --- I have," he added, after he read the question on my face.

Certain thoughts that had lain dormant since I buried my father peaked out of their little coffins in my brain. They had slept in the cemetery of my brain's spiritual sector, next to the mausoleums containing information that the Church had deposited: information about God and Jesus and what it meant to believe in them. It all had become useless information.

But at that very moment I felt the need to dig up that information, unpack it, and compare that information to what this old/young Eskimo was sharing with me. It was as if I were seeing things, understanding things, for the first time. The Church had taught me stories and catechism, but I had never seen the results of anyone who had lived a life of forgiveness. If I had, I'm sure that person would have been as softened as this man was who sat before me. He was sharing with me a response to life I had never learned in "Sunday school" as a kid.

I had met people in Switzerland who lived with every need satisfied and every comfort supplied. I had met people who owned everything that ought to have provided them with happiness and

filled them with love, yet they plodded through life in depression and grief, joyless and without happiness. They were unable to give thanks for the good gifts they had and even complained that they needed more. They were suspicious of non-locals who invaded their villages, and refused to believe that they could be taught something new. They believed that new people, new ideas, or new experiences were to be fought against, not embraced. They were unwilling to open themselves up to the glaciers and mountains in their lives. And so they became stiff and hard-hearted. Their faces were hardened, too. They were not able to listen with their hearts. They could not see with anything other than their physical eyes. They could not open themselves up to life.

"If it is --- an internal change you desire --- you must --- with your heart listen --- and with your heart see," the Eskimo said.

He was reading my mind.

When I lived in the mountains as a child, I felt very close to God, though I never took the time to find out who he really was --- the attributes which made him unique. In fact, though my understanding of him was small, I had many good talks with him. I was very trusting then, until the day I ran down the mountain to get help for my father. On that day I knew my father was seriously injured and I begged God not to let him die. But when I needed God most, he remained silent. When my father died, I felt betrayed and alone. Slowly, I came to the conclusion that God must not exist after all. So I left God behind and only used him as a convenience in times of need.

But in this tiny coffee shop, where an old/young Eskimo with a round face and fiery eyes sat in front of me, God-thoughts emerged from that graveyard in my brain.

"One thing more," the Eskimo said as he waved a hand in front of my glazed eyes. "Satisfied I am also --- because I figured out how to stay warm. Since I have been able to do that, can the rest of these things have been wrong?"

He was a glacier that sat before me. An Eskimo glacier that was of a kind I had never encountered. I had opened myself up to it/him, and it/he played my instrument. Now I would need time to process all of the vibrations that had surged through me.

"Thank you for explaining about the igloos," I said to end the conversation.

He shook my hand. "Well," he said, "I thought --- you would ask about the whale-catchers."

I laughed. "What about the whale-catchers?"

"In my village this season --- we are permitted to strike three whales. By hand we do it. Of course we use every part of the whale we catch --- including the blubber --- the oil --- the bones --- and the skin. After catching a whale --- the whale-catchers --- always pray to the souls of its brothers for forgiveness. Join me in my village in October to hunt the whale --- would you?"

I felt honored to receive such an astonishing invitation. But my plan for October had already been laid out. I would be hunkered down in the wilderness by then. Alaska had called me alone to its interior, and at that very moment a strong impulse instructed me to follow through with that plan.

And just as strong an impulse informed me that killing a whale was an Eskimo need and right, not mine.

But I thanked my coffee companion effusively for the special privilege he extended to me.

"Then a good journey I wish to you," he said as he stood to leave. "On the right path --- I trust --- you are."

I went into town several times after that to get building equipment, and always stopped at Jamie's Health Shop. They made very good coffee there. But I never again saw Mr. Eskimo.

THE FIRST CANOE TRIP

The things Biederman has been through would fill a book. I suppose no man knows more about sled dogs, or winter weather, or making his way alone in wild country.

—Ernie Pyle, 1937 Washington Daily News

During the 1920s and 30s an American named Ed Biederman occupied the foot ledge of a slender dogsled for the majority of his days along the Yukon River, in the interior of Alaska. He was a musher --- a mail deliverer who used a dogsled --- and served an increasing number of demanding traders, hunters and gold seekers who arrived in Alaska during those decades. Ed Biederman's sons, Charlie and Horace, eventually helped with the delivery route and care of the dogs.

If all went well, the 160-mile mail route required six days of travel, one way. Ed Biederman --- and eventually his son, Charlie --- worked the route each winter, completing thirteen roundtrips. In my mind that added up to traveling over four thousand miles of rugged trail a winter.

"My dad, he never believed in stopping to have no tea," Charlie Biederman once said. It was Charlie who made his father, dog-mushing, and the Yukon famous. Charlie, the son, became known as Yukon Charlie.

In Switzerland I read about this family and the true grit they demonstrated as they lived and worked along a temperamental river.

Another book I came across at home was by a daring German

couple who lived in Alaska and used a fold-up Klepper Kayak when they canoed.

(A fold-up kayak! Who would have thought of such a thing? I considered purchasing such a kayak when I got to Alaska, but in the end was very satisfied with the used wooden Old Town Canoe Tobias and I eventually bought. Its well-crafted red cedar plankings, open mahogany gunwales, and shiny brass screws made my artistic heart burn with pride every time we paddled in it. Tobias and I split the $900 cost.)

The German couple wrote about which Alaskan rivers were best to explore, and recommended the Koyukuk for its great variety of scenery. The North Fork of the Koyukuk begins in the rugged Endicott Mountains that are part of the Central Brooks range. From this south edge of the Arctic region the river flows through spacious, glacially sculpted valleys into the Yukon River.

Tobias hadn't read anything. So that left me to decide.

Paddling down the Koyukuk River sounded perfect for a first trip, and I was under the illusion that it wasn't too far north for us to reach without much cost.

The Koyukuk sounded like a good idea until we learned that it was going to be impossible to get to the upper regions of the river for the start of the trip. At that time airplane pilots weren't officially allowed to transport people with their canoes strapped to the skids of the same plane. No pilot we talked to would do it. "If someone notices what I'm doing, he'll report it to the Federal Aviation Administration, and I'll lose my license," each one explained.

So in order to canoe on the Koyukuk, Tobias and I would have to charter two private planes: one for us, and a separate one for our canoe.

That arrangement was going to be way too expensive for our budget, so we searched for another way to another river. We found a river that we could get to by taking two commercial flights: one from Fairbanks to Ft. Yukon, the second from Ft. Yukon to Arctic Village. The canoe would still have to be transported separately, but at least it would be much cheaper than chartering two private

planes.

Arctic Village rests on the east fork of the Chandalar River, one hundred miles north of Fort Yukon and two hundred and ninety miles north of Fairbanks.

Arctic Village would be our starting point.

Before leaving, Tobias and I huddled to figure out what supplies we'd take with us. I needed to hear Tobias' thoughts on the matter. If I did all the planning, maybe I would be making a mistake; maybe I would be forgetting something. I told Tobias that I'd appreciate his help.

"What kind of food do you think we should take?" I asked.

Tobias looked to the ground.

"Well, how about a handful of uncooked rice per person per day?"

Tobias shook the dirt from one of his boots.

"And I think we should bring pasta," I added. "But no vegetables. We can pick fresh greens from the wilderness... Okay?"

Tobias nodded.

"If the canoe capsizes and all the food gets washed away, will we able to survive just by foraging?"

Tobias put his hands in his pockets and shrugged. He had become so used to my lists, my planning, and my way of thinking, that he refused to do any thinking himself. I knew he was not accustomed to having anyone ask for his opinion, but his insecurity was really beginning to annoy me.

I complained to him. "Just once it would be nice to hear what you're thinking, to hear your proposal, to hear an idea different from mine," I said. A little loudly, I might add. If I had gone to Alaska on my own, I would have brought a dog. And now I was beginning to feel like that is just what I had done. I had brought a dog.

Tobias was neither embarrassed nor upset when I ordered him around. He was frightened now that I asked him to get involved in the planning. When I continued with, "What equipment should

we take with us?" his body stiffened. "I don't know what we need," he said hesitantly. "I don't know..." he repeated. Then he added, "You know that." When Tobias felt any pressure coming from the outside, he turned himself inward. During this exchange he almost disappeared.

I was forced to realize that being in Alaska hadn't freed Tobias from stress, it had only permitted him to experience a different kind than what he felt in Switzerland. The stress for him in Alaska came from within, from his lack of confidence in his own abilities.

While building Peter's house, Tobias proved himself to be double-left-handed. When he held an axe or a hammer, the tools or nails would easily find themselves dangerously repositioned. This caused me, as well as Peter and Fabienne, worry for accidents. But no one said anything, and Tobias continued to work slowly and methodically. Tobias' anxiety here in Alaska was also born of his need to find a way out of the chains that had kept his soul imprisoned in St. Gallen. Watching him forced me to remember the reason for his coming on this trip with me: to escape the web that had been suffocating him at home. Tobias told me that before leaving, his mother had shouted at him that he would die in Alaska. I remembered all these things, and backed off.

However, I needed Tobias' input in this one area of wilderness living because Tobias was more experienced at canoeing than I was. He had spent more time on the water than I ever would. This was one thing that was supposed to be very good for his self-esteem, and something I had been counting on for him to take the lead. If I was going to be in charge of the winter, the environment where my expertise lay, couldn't he be in charge of the summer canoe trips?

But I excused him.

Excusing him was easier to do when I reminded myself that in Switzerland, most canoe trips lasted only for a weekend. And a weekend was, at most, three days. If something went wrong, you just had to get in your car --- or hitchhike to get to your car --- to go get help.

In Alaska, there would be no car, no nobody and no nothing. Just mosquitoes. So it was probably good if I prepared myself to

not count on Tobias, after all.

The other supplies we packed for the Chandalar River canoe trip included:

Whole Wheat Grains

Steel Cut Oats

Granola

Sourdough starter in a jar

Dried Eggs

Milk Powder

Cast Iron Skillet (necessary for boiling water and baking bread)

Frying Pan (a treat we bought at the sporting goods store)

Grill (a temptation we succumbed to at the sporting goods store...)

Fishing Gear

Toilet Paper and Shovel (we didn't want to leave any tracks

behind us)

We did not pack water. We decided (I decided) that we'd draw water from the streams and boil it, or we would use the MicroPure tablets we brought from Switzerland to purify it.

In Fairbanks, we strapped our canoe and the majority of our supplies onto the floats of one commercial airplane carrying only cargo, and we strapped ourselves into another commercial plane carrying only passengers. We left Fairbanks on the first Friday in July dressed in jeans and cotton shirts, since we expected the temperatures to stay in the mid-seventies during the day. Of course we understood that they would drop at night, but not much, maybe just down to the low fifties.

With us on our own flight we brought our backpacks with all-weather jackets stuffed inside, our tent and our survival kits. We didn't realize that packing our supply of food with the canoe would be a problem --- until we got to Arctic Village.

When we landed there was no sign of the other plane that carried our canoe and supplies. By late afternoon we still had nothing to

eat but the vegetation growing around us.

Rather than being deflated, I was excited. *Okay. So now it begins,* I thought. *Okay, so now we have to subsist on the land.* Tobias and I started picking plants.

From the far end of the airstrip a construction worker called to us. He climbed down from a piece of heavy construction machinery, sauntered over to us, introduced himself as PeeWee, and wondered "what the heck" we were doing.

PeeWee was charged with the task of building a bigger airstrip for Arctic Village than the one we had landed on. We were foraging on "his" land, didn't we know?

After explaining our situation, PeeWee laughed and invited us to join his men for a welcome soda and a small portion of their bread and vegetables. We thanked them, but accepted only the sodas, since we didn't want to deplete what was apparently rationed food.

After asking for directions into town, we set off, hoping to find some kind of store where we could buy a few food items. Okay, well. Why not look for a store? Surviving was the ability to use all of the resources available at one's disposal.

We walked for about thirty minutes before seeing any houses, then curiously studied their construction. A few of them were built from whole logs, still with rough bark on, and a few more were made from medium-thickness plywood. Most were not in a condition that would keep out cold in winter. The windows and doorways were free of any flowers, and only wild grass grew sparsely on the bumpy patches of land on which the houses were scattered. There were different kinds of detritus lying about in the grass: tires, machine parts, brightly colored plastic containers and metal barrels that had once held oil.

"It's so...um...dirty," Tobias whispered, echoing my own thoughts. And he added, "So... ugly."

At that moment I remembered fragments of the conversation I had had with the Eskimo in Fairbanks.

Before the Westerners came, our people lived underground.

Now I was looking at Eskimo houses above ground...houses that

lacked evidence of hundreds of years' worth of building knowledge that Westerners put to use when they build.

Our lives were not about accumulating things. We gave back to the earth what it had given to us.

Was all this "stuff" in the yards evidence of giving back?

Our tools and our clothes could be left to disintegrate if we no longer needed them.

Were they leaving their "stuff" in the open, expecting it to disintegrate?

Only at this moment, walking through Arctic Village, did I begin to understand the difficulties an Alaska Native might have adjusting to a modern world.

If a modern and powerful government preaches to a shy and humbled people that it is "smart" to live above ground, could these shy and humble people contradict this "smarter" intelligence?

If an Alaska Native were given tools made of metal and plastic, would he automatically know how to operate these tools so they wouldn't break down easily? Had he been given any real training in how to dispose of metal and plastic?

An Alaska Native had been schooled by his tradition that it was perfectly acceptable for him to place outside of his dwelling tools that were no longer usable. He understood that if they were totally exposed to the elements they could disintegrate, and be given back to the tundra.

No one had taught him that plastic doesn't disintegrate. No one had taught him how to dispose of metal oil barrels, or if needed, how to preserve them, because well-cared-for metal barrels could last and be reused for many, many years.

So perhaps the front and back yards of these Arctic Village dwellings looked like junkyards not because their owners were dirty, but because the owners had come from a culture that had instilled in them a different kind of habit.

On the road from a distance Tobias and I saw men in their yards working on boats or bikes, or tampering with their fishing equipment. The closer we got to the yards, however, we noticed

that these same men were quietly disappearing.

From behind the window shades of a log house on the left, a few heads peeked out. The same thing happened in the plywood house on the right. But no one came out to talk to us.

And we found no store.

When we reached the end of the road, there was one Alaska Native standing at the doorway of his house, staring at us suspiciously.

"Is there a store here where we can buy something to eat?" I asked.

The Native didn't answer right away, but directed his gaze past me. "No," he finally coughed up. "You can't buy anything here."

Our traditions taught us to care for those who were without --- who were in need. If there was someone traveling in the wilderness --- we shared what heat and shelter and food we had. That was our custom.

The Eskimo's words came back to me and I didn't know what to do with them. Had the White Man changed the Alaska Natives so completely?

In my entire life I had never felt as unwelcomed as I did during those moments. I sensed we were a disturbance --- a terrible disruption in the daily life of this tiny town.

After walking fifteen minutes away from the village, we found a protected spot by the river to put up our tent. We were fifteen minutes away from the village and fifteen minutes away from the airport. Two days later someone from the village sent two young girls to tell us the plane with our canoe had arrived.

The girls stayed at a safe distance. There were no smiles on their faces. They held each other's hands, swatted away some mosquitoes, and then left.

I was hoping I could have talked with the Athabascans there in Arctic Village. I was looking forward to a conversation about their view of the isolated world in which they lived. I was ready to listen to what their spirits could impart to me, and to learn what they had to teach me.

But I left Arctic Village with an emptiness in my soul.

| 16 |

ON THE CHANDALAR RIVER

owever, there were so very many other things to fill it up again.

The immenseness of Alaska was mesmerizing. We continued down the Chandalar, sometimes in fast water, thrilling to its movement. There were glorious mountains in the distance, and only a quiet hum of insects all around. We wore long-sleeved shirts buttoned at the wrist and fixed with Velcro tape at the neck, wrists, and bottom of the shirt. The mosquitoes were worse than we expected. Even so, I stopped using the super-duper bug spray. I hated breathing in all those chemicals and having the exposed parts of my body (face and hands) absorb the poisons. Tobias, like me, began to not even feel the stings after a while. Actually the mosquitoes did not attack us while we paddled on the water. They converged when we went ashore. Sometimes our faces were black because of the thickness of their swarms. Nevertheless, the thrill of seeing any wild creature kept us going ashore again and again.

One day during one of our stops I climbed over a small hill to find an Arctic fox digging around in the underbrush. He was no more than two feet long from his head to the beginning of his tail, and his fur was totally black. The tail added about another foot of bushy blackness to its length. The fox's muzzle and legs were short, making him look cute, like a house pet. I believe he heard my steps because he was already looking in my direction as I came over the mound. I stopped. He had found a nest of bird eggs. One egg was in his mouth.

I backed away, and lowered my body to the ground on the other side of the hill. The fox did not follow me. So I crawled back up to the rise to watch the fox finish his project. Using a thick paw, he buried two eggs under a pile of dirt and leaves, saving them to eat for a later time.

Tobias and I continued our journey by following the river wherever it took us. We were a good team in the canoe. Tobias manned the back. The boatman with the most experience always sits in the back of the canoe, and Tobias took his position after I directed him to do so. It was the right place for him. He was the most experienced. I worked to match his skillful paddling, and we would give each other high fives after successfully conquering white water on the Chandalar. By day we looked for interesting places to hike inland, and at night we stopped to sleep.

Before stopping we would scan the shore, looking out for the best place to make camp. What did we look for? We were quite picky, really, and wouldn't stay just anywhere. We almost never stayed at the first place we spotted. On the Chandalar we trained our eyes to recognize where others had been before, probably during the time of the Gold Rush. We knew others had camped in these sites by the way the brush or vegetation had been reordered.

You can be trained to recognize human intervention, too, if you've ever noted how a forest rebuilds itself after a fire. Once the flames have died, once the scorched and damaged tall trees have fallen and scarred the land around them, the first plants that will rise up out of the ground will be small leafy bushes. These will rise up and become leaf trees. Needle trees require the fallen leaves from the bush trees as fertilizer in order to grow. Needle trees rise up only after bush trees sprout and shed some of their leaves. Northern pine trees have thin trunks and grow very slowly. I measured one that was only about eight inches across, yet it had over two hundred rings. A tree with a diameter of eight inches across was two hundred years old! Because of permafrost, northern pines have a hard life and must be very sturdy to survive such a long time. People who camp along a river need wood for fires to cook and warm themselves, so they cut down the sturdy pinewood, which burns longer than wood from bush trees.

So Tobias and I looked out for flat pieces of shoreline where only smaller bush trees were thriving in place of the tall pines that had been cut down by some former trespasser. We chose not to destroy or use any tall living pine trees. We would burn only scavenged dead wood.

What defined a good campsite?

First, it had to be flat with protective, leafy bushes and a swath of grass low enough and soft enough to sit or lie upon. Second, it had to be close to the river, because we needed an accessible source of water and we always appreciated a good view! And finally, it had to be higher than the riverbank, because if a storm came unexpectedly in the night, we didn't want to get washed away in a flood.

During a thunderstorm in the mountains of Switzerland, a river's water level can rise a couple of meters, or more than six feet. If a camper stays right on the riverbank he can easily get swept away.

The same thing could have been possible on the Chandalar, because the Chandalar's headwaters begin in the Brooks Range, the highest mountain range in the Arctic Circle.

A couple of times we ignored our last rule and camped low along the riverbank. We might have been testing our luck, but we had come to know when no storm was brewing.

One night while camping low to the river against our better judgment, the fire had just settled down to a nice steady glow, the sleeping floor was swept clean, and my sleeping bag was unrolled and inviting.

After sliding into it and just before drifting off, I murmured, "Tobias, if there's a thunderstorm up in the mountains, I guess we'll just have to get swept away. Wake me up if you start swimming in your dreams."

I was in deep slumber when the shouting started.

"AAAY!!!! We're going to get swept away!"

Startled, I sat up. The fire was still glowing. I felt around me. Everything was dry.

"Tobias," I called across to him, "you're dreaming!"

"No! There's water! There's water everywhere! It's coming! It's here!

It's all over us," Tobias screamed.

Still feeling all around me with one hand, I untangled myself from my sleeping bag. Tobias' hands were flailing and his eyes were open. But there was no water. Everything was dry.

I told him a second time --- then a third --- that he was dreaming. He looked at me with wide eyes, then all of a sudden, dropped back down to his sleeping bag, went right back to sleep, and began to snore.

After that I understood the power suggestion alone had over Tobias. Offhand words or rash looks from another person could penetrate the deep recesses of his mind, even though it appeared he hadn't even noticed them.

But why did he let this happen? How could anyone be so affected by an off-hand remark?

When I asked this question of myself, memories of the night that Tobias had invited me to dinner with him and his parents came flooding back. Perhaps answers could be found in those memories?

At that dinner I had watched, speechless, as Mrs. Senn manipulated control over her son with not just words, but with looks, too. Her gazes weren't full of encouragement; they were full of disappointment, belittlement, and rejection. One raised eyebrow and one shake of the head ever-so-slightly could cause the muscles in Tobias' face to tighten and all the air to escape from his lungs. Her pursed lips and squinty eyes, rolled up to the left or right at just the right time, even made me feel inadequate, childish, or stupid for the ideas I was expressing. Many times that night, as Tobias endured each judgmental stare, as his face tightened and the air escaped from his lungs, his body sank in upon itself. He was physically disappearing. Eventually his spirit turned inward, and by the end of the meal he wasn't responding to anyone.

As I thought about that experience during the-night-by-the river-with-no-floodwater, I figured that Tobias probably had never challenged his mother whenever she gave him disapproving looks. Because if he had, I concluded, I would have witnessed something different at the dinner table that night. But neither

Tobias nor his father nor his mother cleared the air. Not one of them spoke the truth about what he or she was really thinking.

That night on the river I also figured that Tobias probably had trouble grasping or defining what he needed to challenge.

He could not answer an accusation from his mother because nothing had been spoken. If Mrs. Senn had said the word "stupid," Tobias could have questioned her, "How am I stupid? What did I do? What could I have done?" Not strong enough to understand, not strong enough to climb out from under the barrage of looks, Tobias waited for words that never came. Since Mrs. Senn never explained herself, Tobias could never challenge her. He could never confront her. He was left to lick his wounds all by himself.

Later on in the-night-by-the river-with-no-floodwater, I was reminded of the times I had become impatient with Tobias because he offered so little of himself or shared so little of his thoughts. I asked myself how many times had I given him a disapproving look? How many times had I become irritated with him because he was so ill-equipped to handle himself in nature? How many times had I tried to dispel my irritation by making remarks that I considered humorous but in fact were cutting --- made to laugh at him rather than with him --- and probably just made him feel clumsier than he already felt?

When he handled a tool incorrectly, even foolishly, what words or looks had I given him?

After Tobias' nightmare on the river, I resolved to remember the harm his mother had already caused him through years of pregnant looks, and to alter my behavior.

Insight into Tobias came to me because I grew up in a similar situation with my father.

A certain set of circumstances would occur. I would see them one way, my father would see them another. And no matter what happened, no matter how I saw things, my father insisted his viewpoint was always the correct one. As a child I had very little confidence in my ability to assess whether my personal convictions were right or wrong because my father continually insisted I was wrong, every time.

If I did something to displease my father, he would not tell me what I had done. His usual punishment was silence. So I would suffer the silence.

Once, when I was about eight years old, I was playing outside our house in Kreuzlingen. During those days my father would come home by bicycle for lunch, and on this particular day I stopped my play and began to look for him. As he parked his bike, I stood and waved hello to him, happy to see him. My father gave no response, rushed into the house, then closed the door behind him. He didn't speak to me for two weeks after that.

Had I made a terrible mistake, broken something, done something horribly wrong?

My mother didn't tell me right away what it was. A day or two later she finally explained, "Your father is angry that you didn't say hello to him."

"But I did ---" Even now I can feel my face light up and see my hand waving while saying "Hello, Vati."

Mueti wasn't listening.

And Vati hadn't seen and hadn't heard. There was no compunction within him that forced him to consider the possibility that he might have been wrong.

A father can respond to a disagreement in a number of ways. He can say, "I'm sorry I didn't see you." Or, "You were speaking in such a low voice I couldn't hear you." Or, "Next time, can you stop playing when you see me?" But he never said any of these things, and his silence happened time and time again for things I had no idea I had done wrong. Time and again he ignored me for things that he later said I did that I hadn't done!

When a father doesn't talk to his child for an extended amount of time, it is quite traumatic for the child.

If Tobias and I located a good spot for our camp, we landed and pulled our canoe ashore where it wouldn't be washed away. Then I would unload my backpack. In the backpack I carried one change of clothes which was always wrapped separately in plastic to keep

it dry, my first aid kit, a parka for warmth, and a poncho to protect from the rain. Strapped to the side of the backpack was an axe.

Inside the canoe we traveled with army-made waterproof sacks in which we kept sleeping bags, therma-rest mattresses, extra clothes, food, and the tent. The sacks were made from a fabric a little thinner than fabric used to make boat sails, and the insides were lined with rubber. The sacks had a circle bottom.

Whoever carried the rubberized bags onto shore was usually the one to start setting up the tent. Whoever brought the cooking pans and the grill from the canoe was the one to start gathering sticks for the fire. I knew we were fancy carrying a grill. The grill was a luxury to have in the wilderness. We bought it in a large hardware store in Fairbanks (along with the army-made waterproof sacks). At that time there were no giant hardware stores in Switzerland. Swiss stores were small and minimally stocked with a few nails, nuts and screws. So whenever we went into a huge store like the REI in Fairbanks, Tobias and I were often carried away by all the choices we had. (The reason you may note more items for our "survival" than previously listed.)

I never minded hunting for firewood, because it always provided the opportunity to think and to explore. Often I would meander around looking here and there, always with eyes open for any unusual movement, any telltale sign or sound of other creatures that would be interesting to watch.

The lynx is a creature that rarely shows itself to humans. It hunts at night, which makes any opportunity for a human to observe it all the more difficult. It will eat mice, squirrels and birds, but prefers the snowshoe hare. Because of their golden brown fur sprinkled with dark spots, lynx have the ability to make themselves invisible. All the more incredible that one crossed my path one day.

One evening, passing through a not too thickly wooded birch forest, I came upon a very useable log of fallen dead wood for the evening campfire. Reaching down to saddle the log onto my back, I glimpsed a swath of burnished fur pass about thirty feet ahead. The log remained where it was and I stood erect. Detecting my movement, the lynx halted, too. His long tufts of black hair jutting from the tips of his ears made him look as surprised to see me as I was to see him.

We stared at each other without moving. After what was at least

a full minute, the lynx satisfied his curiosity, and turned his head away. Slowly he lifted a huge paw covered in thick fur, placed it on the ground in front of him, and crept silently on in the direction he was headed. I exhaled slowly, then saddled the almost forgotten log over my shoulders.

Back at the campsite, Tobias was attending to the boring job of setting up the tent. I told him I would go down to the river to catch fish for dinner, and knew Tobias would gather plants to make a salad. Sharing camping responsibilities always went smoothly. The work wasn't exciting, but it needed to be done. I thought about how different this was to my experience working in an office.

In an office, people rarely share the communal responsibilities equally. There are always the same people who clean up, and the same others who don't clean up.

Repetitive jobs and cleaning up in any office make for boring, thankless work.

In a design studio, the boring work is making the final drawings. Mr. Muller-Brockmann was specific and demanding in letter-spacing. I worked at MBD before desktop publishing software existed, and everything had to be done manually. You had to paste up a layout by selecting blocks of type and sometimes cut paragraphs apart line by line. Or letter by letter. Some people I worked with didn't want to do the separating work because they didn't understand typographic rules. Others didn't want to cut apart body type because it was too tedious, instead desiring to do the fast, effortless, creative work. Older guys, who had worked at the company for years had more rights than I, the new kid, so they didn't ever have to do the boring work of cutting apart the type.

Sometimes the older guys who do the fun, creative stuff, never actually see the final drawings, and so never have the opportunity to check and make sure that their designs work.

I recall an architectural job done for the train station in Avignon, France. The train station is a beautiful building, but the architect forgot to consider the purpose of a train station, and designed the train platforms to stand exposed in the open air. Now in Avignon, when passengers wait for their trains, they get wet when it rains, they get hot when the sun pours down, and they get cold when it's

cold outside.

Charles-Édouard Jeanneret, better known as Le Corbusier, was a Swiss-French architect who is very famous for the Notre Dame du Haut, a church he designed in a town called Ronchamp, France. The church's whitewashed exterior walls curve and swell with what look like only pinpoint windows. But inside, deep window recesses open up into wide pathways that reflect the sun's rays. The whole effect produces in the interior an ethereal, mystic light. A church is for the purposes of concentration, meditation and even for evoking an emotional response from the spiritual. For many, the Notre Dame du Haut accomplishes these purposes. The church is an example of a successful design. On this design Le Corbusier must have done the tedious work of the final drawings. He must have set up the tent and gathered the wood and set up the grill. He must have checked his form against function. But Le Corbusier is most frequently known for a home he designed in Poissy, France, commissioned by the Savoye family. After being built it was found to have many mechanical and structural problems, letting in rain and cold. Le Corbusier ignored pleas to fix these problems and the family never really moved in. Apparently Le Corbusier had not done, or even supervised, the detail work and the home eventually had to be torn apart and rebuilt.

Doing the grunt work, occupying oneself with the boring details, helps a person make sure that the final design will come out properly. Sometimes it's painless to come up with the big design, but the genius (and the real work) is in making the result functional, as well as aesthetically pleasing.

Setting up the tent, building the fire, doing the cooking --- these were the tasks that enabled our trip along the Chandalar to be enjoyable, comfortable, and interesting, rather than irritating, difficult or dangerous. We were always hungry when we stopped to camp for the night. During the day finger foods sufficed. A few nuts, a few dried fruits. We would pause along the river not so much to have lunch, because lunch was not our main objective. We paused to hike into the woods. We were always on the lookout for what new animal we could see, what new place we could experience.

One of the last things required when setting up camp was to determine where to locate the "outhouse".

We always dug far away from the camping area, and often succeeded in constructing a comfortable seat for the toilet out of wood branches and smooth, round stones.

I carried with me one question always: Did I have the right to leave my tracks behind? In other words, did I have the right to leave evidence of my presence in the wilderness? Canoeing down the Chandalar was not something I had to do to survive; I chose to travel half way around the world to experience the land and the space of Alaska. I committed to this adventure as a personal challenge, to prove that proper preparation facilitates success in surviving anywhere. Did I have the right to change something about the landscape through which I passed? Was my presence harming the area in some way? Tobias and I decided to leave every place where we stopped in the same condition we found it, as much as possible. If there was grass on the ground in the area of the chosen campsite, then grass was cut away before building the fire, and prior to leaving, the grass was replaced. Perhaps nature wouldn't be harmed if we didn't leave too many tracks behind, and made every effort to cover them before we left.

But not leaving any tracks didn't mean that our presence in the wilderness went unnoticed. One morning our canoe slid through a shallow part of the Chandalar and approached a moose calf taking a bath. The calf's bronze fur glistened in the sun, and over long spindly legs its little body rocked back and forth near the river's shore. It was when his oversized head leaned down to the water that he caught a glimpse of us. Even from a distance his eyes looked huge, bigger than golf balls. We were fascinated as the calf stepped inquisitively towards us. Then out of nowhere a cow moose leaped into view. I stopped my paddle stroke in midair. Tobias stuck his paddle into the river, and managed to halt the movement of the canoe. We were about two hundred feet from the animals. The moose did not charge. But I was still amazed at the swiftness with which she had sprung out of nowhere to stride in between us and her baby. When the moose saw that Tobias and I were not coming closer, she turned and nudged her calf out of the water and into the woods.

| 17 |

VENETIE

We spent many satisfying days like this on the river, purposely staying away from any other human contact. But after the second week, our supply of coffee, an important and necessary ingredient to our well-being, had been depleted.

After checking the map we started looking out for Venetie, the nearest Alaskan Native village on the Chandalar River. A wide, flat landing area for boats seemed good evidence that the town could be above us, and we decided to stop.

As we steered our canoe to shore, a young Alaska Native appeared at the riverbank's steep edge. He was maneuvering a canoe of his own above his head, and then slid it down the riverbank to the water. Noticing that we were coming ashore, he advised us to guard our canoe, warning that, if left unattended, kids from town might take it out, not be able to control it, jump into the river, and let it get washed away. So Tobias volunteered to keep guard of the boat while I went up to town to purchase some coffee.

In Europe there is a definite structure to villages and towns. For instance, a church is often built at the center, and frequently placed on the highest elevation of the land. Shops and restaurants fan out around the church, and then houses fan out around the shops and restaurants. In some cities, the church might not be at the center, but there is some significant structure to mark the center, around which commerce and the shops of life are located. European towns were built in order for people to be able to protect themselves.

I found no such structure to Alaskan Native towns. A road ran through Venetie, but from all appearances, the houses must have existed before the road.

It was around noon and, remembering what kind of unfriendly souls we encountered in Arctic Village, I tried to make myself invisible until I found a store. I spotted an old man sitting outside one of the houses. His shuttered eyes formed two oblique lines on either side of a tanned and chiseled face. He was wearing a long-sleeve shirt with a faded design, and his long hands were draped over the arm rests of his porch chair. I tried to sneak past him.

"Hey, you!" he called out to me. "Come over and talk to me!" I didn't think I had made any noise. Perhaps this old man felt my spirit.

I walked closer to his porch.

"What are you doing?" he asked.

"Looking to buy some coffee," I answered. He considered that a moment.

"And where did you come from?" he asked.

"Switzerland," I answered.

The furrows on his forehead deepened.

"But why are you *here*?" he asked insistently.

His tone was friendly, and because he spoke English as I do --- not using so many words --- I felt an immediate connection with him. "So you want me to tell you my story?" I asked.

He pointed to the porch step with a bony brown finger. "You can sit down," he said.

I sat on the top step with my backpack still on.

"A friend and I are taking a canoe trip down the Chandalar River..." I began.

When I finished, the old man closed his dark eyes and nodded. When I told him I had a few questions for him, the slits fluttered open quickly and the creases in his face broadened into a smile. His gums were healthy and his teeth were clean.

"Where are *you* from?" I asked.

He told me he had been a nomad when he was young. He and his father and mother and sister trundled from place to place, east and west and south of Venetie, tracking the migration of caribou and moose herds. His family lived off of the rewards of their hunting as well as the berries and roots that grew in the taiga and on the tundra.

He told me that he had come to the village twenty years before. "I settled here when it was part of Reservation land. I thought I'd stay only for a while. But about the time I was planning to move on, the American government started saying that this land here around Venetie had to become part of the state of Alaska. They didn't want it to be a reservation anymore."

Now he started tapping his fingers on the wooden arms of the chair. And he looked at me as if he were having the same conversation he had had ten years or so before.

"Oh yes, they offered to pay us for the land. But if we took the money, then they would take away any of our future claims to it. If we took their money we wouldn't be able to stop them from digging or drilling or cutting down our trees. We could live on the land, but they would have the right to do what they wanted to it."

He lifted a thumb and with it indicated somewhere behind his head. "You said you stopped in Arctic Village up there on the Chandalar?"

I scratched my beard. This was an opportunity to tell him exactly what happened in Arctic Village. "Yes, we ---"

"Well, people from Arctic Village and Christian Village and Robert's Fish Camp united together to decide whether to keep this land or sell it to the American government. I stayed to help figure out what we should do. The old people in the villages didn't want to lose possession of property they felt they had a sacred right to, even though the government promised to pay them a lot of money for it. Some of the rest of the people argued that we should keep the land because land will always be useful and will always be with us. And then there were others who wanted the money." He shook his head. "I shook my head a lot at them because

I didn't understand. 'If we take the money,' I said to them, 'if we take the money, what'll we do with it?' So I helped them decide." He strummed the arm rests and was silent.

I was distracted by a small group of men who had gathered around the old man's porch to get a good look at me, the foreigner who had dropped in from outer space. They all started whispering among themselves. One of the men spoke up. "Who wanted the money, Mr. Henry? Who?" he asked.

I could tell that this was a story that had been told many times.

"You know who wanted the money," Mr. Henry answered with an easy laugh. He looked at each man in the group. "You all know who wanted the money. That's enough of that. And anyway," he said tipping his forehead my way, "it's this fella here that I was sharing the story with."

"So," I asked him, "what did you decide?"

"We didn't take the money. Now this land is still ours."

"Well," I said, "except for the mosquitoes," and then I added in a lower voice, "and a few unfriendly souls up north..." But I didn't finish the sentence. They all looked at me blankly. So I repeated the first part. "Except for the mosquitoes, all of your land is like paradise to me," I said.

Mr. Henry smiled. "Like paradise," he repeated. Then he sighed and admitted, "We do have our problems."

I thought he was going to mention his brothers in Arctic Village as one of the problems, but instead he pointed to my backpack. "Venetie is a dry place," he said. "No alcohol." And just in case I didn't get the message, he extended a long bony thumb toward his mouth and imitated taking a drink from a bottle. He shook his head. "Cannot drink it, cannot bring it in." His stare bore a hole into my backpack.

I laughed and said the only thing I carried in my backpack at the moment was a thermos of water.

The old man then told me they had to enforce this policy in the village because alcohol had caused a lot of devastation among Alaska Natives.

I told him I understood because of what I had seen in Anchorage.

"Our Village Chief does a very good job of enforcing this policy," he explained. "I'm just trying to make his job a little easier today." And then with a hint of a smile he asked, "Would you like to meet him?"

I assured him I would.

A young man from the gathered group that had been listening intently to our conversation ran to bring the Village Chief, who soon trotted to the porch wearing jeans, a work shirt and sneakers. When he extended his hand, I shook it.

"So you've been speaking to my father?" he asked with a welcoming smile.

"Yes, I guess I have," I answered.

Then the Village Chief, Mr. Henry, Junior, invited me to stay for lunch.

Poor Tobias still stood guard at the river. I had been talking for over two hours.

Chairs set up in a circle inside the house of the old man soon became comfortably occupied by men and women of the village who heard --- through the village grapevine --- about me, the new visitor in town. Quickly the house began to feel like a home. There was a distinct age difference among the men and women there. The village elders, whose teeth and gums were strong, sat tall in their chairs with strength in their legs and chests. The middle-aged men were less-healthy looking, having been beaten down by life, or alcohol. Their teeth were rotting from the sugar they consumed and their faces reflected an unhappiness and wantonness that manifests after years of alcohol consumption. I studied the face of each person as the food for lunch was placed on the table in the middle of the room. During the meal the Village Chief spoke proudly about the school they had in town and the electricity that diesel-powered generators were providing to some of the houses.

Out of nowhere one of the neighbors brought his daughter before me. She was probably nineteen or twenty, wearing jeans and a cowgirl shirt with metal buttons. Her long, black hair gleamed,

and the smile on her smooth, clear face was sweet. She sat next to me and asked me a few questions about my trip. I asked her about the university where she was studying to become a teacher. The girl's father watched us as we talked. Seeing that we were getting along, he got up from his seat and walked over to stand in front of us.

"Do you like her?" he asked me, pointing to the girl with the shiny buttons and hair.

"Sure I do," I answered. "She seems like a very nice person."

"You can have her," he said, bending down and looking into my face.

I thought it was a joke and turned to the daughter next to me to see if she was smiling.

The daughter stared straight ahead. Her body was tight with discomfort.

"You can marry her," the father said when I turned back to him. Some of the other adults in the room heard him and smiled shyly.

I...I was taken aback. He was serious. Maybe the father thought that any life I could offer his daughter would be better than the bleak future he saw for her in his village, school or no, alcohol or no. I was humbled and saddened. I bowed my head, not sure of how to decline the offer without offending the father or the girl. Finally I just decided to tell them the truth, however inadequate. I told them that I had a friend with whom I was travelling, and that there would not be room enough in the canoe for a third person to join us. My journey here into the interior of Alaska was not purposed for choosing a wife. This was a journey for something else completely. It would have taken much too long to explain all of that.

What made my answer a little more acceptable, I hoped, was observing that I had chosen dried salmon instead of grilled caribou meat for lunch. The father raised his eyebrows and a slow grin came across his face. The other men in the room pointed to the fish. "Squaw candy," they said and laughed. "Fish is for the women," one of them explained in case I didn't understand. And finally a few of them offered advice I had heard from others in

Anchorage and Fairbanks. "Men must eat real meat to survive in Alaska." They meant it for my good. But that day the salmon I had for lunch was very tasty, and I was quite satisfied.

When lunch was finished, I shook hands with the old man who had invited me onto his porch and into his life, and the old man hugged me. He gave me his address so that I might keep in touch with him.

I knew I had stayed a long time in Venetie without sending word to Tobias. I knew he would be worried because I had been gone for so long. And I also knew he would be angry when I showed up and told him I had been having lunch and visiting with the people of the town. I had thought about stepping away from the village to let Tobias know what I was doing. But I didn't want to stop the feeling or the flow of all those interactions on that marvelous afternoon. I didn't want to cut short the time in Venetie before my stay was supposed to end. And anyway, if I left to tell Tobias he should come up to the village from the river, who would watch the canoe?

The other side of the coin was that I had a kind of anger brewing inside of me. Having Tobias around me all the time was beginning to make me feel claustrophobic, and my hike up to Venetie was an escape. It was an experience I wanted just for myself.

Of course it was selfish.

When I got back to him, I told him, "Now it's your turn to go up to the village." But Tobias had no desire to do so.

18

THE CRAZY SWISS

The Chandalar joins the Yukon River where the Yukon bends and its waters begin to flow southwesterly. So at the Yukon bend, we, too, began traveling southwesterly through a floodplain out of which have emerged islands of plant and animal life. We recognized this part of the river as the Yukon Flats, which gave us the impression that we were riding in a maze of braided streams. Where would the stream we had chosen come out at the other end? We had to pay attention to the currents, always feeling for the strong force of the main river. Surrounding us were undulating countryside, spruce, birch and aspen trees, and lots and lots of canvasback ducks and ducklings. At night we heard loons in the distance, but never were able to spot any during the day.

One evening along the Yukon, we climbed high upon an upland ridge to set up camp. From our lofty perch we could see for miles around. I felt like a bird myself. It was a freeing feeling, after being so many hours in a canoe and low to the ground.

In the morning we enjoyed scrambled eggs, freshly-baked bread, self-made jam, and freshly brewed coffee flavored with some milk reconstituted from powder. After breakfast we sat back to watch the slow movement of the river. A bald eagle circled above our heads. Suddenly he propelled himself straight for the water and just as quickly flew up in a circle away from us. Evidently the eagle had spotted a fat fish near the water's surface because he swooped to the same place a second, and then a third time. On its third swoop, the eagle's powerful

talons hooked a squirming salmon. The eagle tried to lift, but couldn't. The fish fought to escape, but couldn't do that either. No matter how hard the salmon fought, the eagle would not let go of his prey. He dragged that salmon through the water, struggling again and again to lift its wings. All of a sudden it gave up trying to fly and started to swim, stroking with its feathered appendages. We laughed and figured the eagle must have been very hungry. Finally the bird reached the shoreline, and dragged the fish out of the water. The fish flopped up a few times, and then lay immobile. At last the bald eagle would have his breakfast, too.

Then, there it was, floating slowly down the river: one of those motorboats that you see on a lake or canal close to the coast of Florida. It was a big, fancy, private fishing boat that no one would ever expect to see on a river in Alaska. I pulled out my binoculars to see who was onboard and detected one lone person. What was he doing? Why wasn't he using his engine?

Tobias and I shouted and waved our arms.

The boatman heard our shouts and looked our way. He started the engine and came back upstream toward us.

Tobias and I scrambled down the riverbank. After he threw us his line and we pulled the craft in, the compact, muscular skipper jumped ashore. He was wearing jeans, boots, a short sleeve shirt, and a worn look on his face. No hat covered his graying hair. We soon learned that his engine had just used the last fumes from his fuel tank to reach us. The boatman was trying to get as far down the river as he could by floating, hoping to reach Stevens Village where he could buy more fuel. His name was Leo.

We invited Leo to breakfast.

He told us he was from Florida (!) and that he and a friend were searching for gold. They had put their boat in the water at Circle City, an old mining town at the end of Steese Highway on the Yukon River, south of Fort Yukon, where they had left a car. They planned to travel along the Yukon north to the Porcupine River, along which they intended to hunt for gold.

They never expected to have problems with the boat's motor. However, when the problems surfaced, the friend left the boat to

return to Circle City, pick up the car, and meet Leo later at the Yukon Bridge. From there they would ride by truck to Fairbanks to get help to resolve the boat's problems. So instead of going northeast, the boat was now floating southwest.

After breakfast, Leo left us to continue on his float trip down to Stevens Village, and we leisurely packed up our camp. Sometime later we unexpectedly again met up with Leo and his boat, because both had been swept into the wrong ribbon of the river. The water was shallow and the current was weak. Leo was going nowhere. The boat was stuck. Tobias and I offered to pull Leo's boat out to the wider arm of the Yukon.

Leo was doubtful. Two young men in a canoe pulling a big fishing boat --- upstream? But he had nothing to lose for trying.

He threw us his ropes.

Tobias and I created a bit of sweat as we pulled and paddled, but eventually we were able to set Leo on the right arm of the Yukon and head him in the direction of Stevens Village. Hopefully there he could fill up his boat with the fuel it needed to carry him down to the Yukon Bridge. To show his appreciation he offered to give us a ride back to Fairbanks from the Yukon Bridge, if we wanted to go with him. We thanked him kindly and told him that if we got to the bridge on time, we'd accept his offer, otherwise we'd find another way. Dalton Highway, which crosses over the Yukon River by way of the Yukon Bridge, is a fairly busy thoroughfare and we figured we'd have lots of opportunities to ask a truck driver about the possibility of putting our canoe on his truck and hitching a ride back to Fairbanks. We didn't want to rush ourselves, or our trip, by promising to be at the bridge at a specific day or time. Surely Leo would have arrived there and departed before we got even close.

But when we reached the Yukon Bridge, there was Leo's friend, still waiting for Leo and the boat to reach the meeting point.

Leo's friend leaned nonchalantly against his truck, which was attached to a camper, while he looked out over the water. Next to the camper sat a pile of camping equipment, two canoes and four hikers. When we carried our supplies and canoe up to the road where Leo's friend and the group loitered, our ears started

burning. The four hikers were speaking Swiss-German, and they also were waiting for Leo. There were three girls who were friends, and a guy who was the boyfriend of one of the girls. They had met Leo further up the Porcupine River. Tobias and I learned pretty quickly that they were crazy people. They complained that over the course of their two-week journey they had lost many hours of sleep because they had set up bear-watches every night. Two of them would stay awake each night, walking around with guns.

During our cruise down the Chandalar I never had a fear of animals attacking Tobias and me at night. I simply trusted that animals wouldn't come to harm us. Wild animals instinctively stay at a distance from human beings, for whom they have a natural fear. Some animals can be aggressive, but usually only when provoked. Plus, I had my whistle. I bought it at the sporting goods store in Anchorage. It was a long, sleek piece of smooth silver with a loud and shrill sound to scare off even the fiercest bear. The whistle was a beauty. I bought it just in case. Just in case my theory about bears turned out to be just that...a theory, and not a principle.

On one of our daily hikes in the Yukon Flats area I did notice bear tracks leading away from the river. Tobias and I followed them. We very quickly came across an ant hill that had been torn apart, which was fresh evidence of at least one grizzly in the woods. Bodily waste from bears, called bear scat, was abundant a few feet from the ant hill. Tobias became anxious. I did, too. I was anxious to see a live grizzly, and study him from a safe distance. We found the bear in a leafy glen, slurping on some mushrooms. It was blond and fat, and very big. Bigger than I, and no doubt three times my weight. Tobias and I kept our distance, and the bear never noticed us. There you go. My theory worked as fact. And I never even had to use the whistle.

But as for those four crazy Swiss, we found they weren't too bad at all when we got to know them. We had plenty of time for that, after we all piled into Leo's large camper for the drive back to Fairbanks. We had a flat tire along the way, but otherwise, it didn't take us long at all --- not quite eight hours.

GUSTAV, ELISABETH, & RENTING A CANOE

eo dropped us off at the Tanana Campground, the first place Tobias and I stayed when we arrived in Fairbanks, and the place where the other Swiss campers had decided to overnight. Peter, Fabienne and her little blond daughter, Petra, came to retrieve us, interrupting the middle of their work day.

After unloading our packs, Tobias and I, curious to see the progress done on the log cabin during the weeks we had been away, joined Peter and Fabienne at the construction site. It now hosted two other volunteers: Peter's brother, Gustav, and Gustav's wife, Elisabeth. Gustav, trained as a surgeon, would adapt his deftness with surgical tools to the heavy axes and saws we were using and help with the building. And I assumed Elisabeth, a licensed physiotherapist who performed cranial-sacral manipulation and grief therapy, was there to offer her muscle power as well.

But as all the men took up their designated building tasks and Fabienne busied herself with tending to Petra, Elisabeth said she would "help in the garden". A short while later, from high up on my log perch, I saw her lying in the furrows. Wondering what she was doing, I called to her to ask.

"Listening to hear if the carrots are growing," she answered.

When Peter whispered to me that Elisabeth was in early pregnancy and had low blood pressure, I let her continue to listen.

At the evening meal Peter and Fabienne asked a few questions about our recent canoe trip and their interest was satisfied with a few short stories of our time away.

Gustav and Elisabeth, however, were very curious about everything Tobias and I had done for the previous three weeks. Gustav was a white-water rafter, and had completed many rafting jaunts in Switzerland. In fact, rafting was one of the things he and Elisabeth had come to Alaska to do.

Gustav asked Tobias and me if we'd like to join them on a canoe trip that he and Elisabeth had originally planned to do on their own. But after considering that Tobias and I had already been "out there," I think Gustav thought it wasn't a bad idea to have a couple of guys along who knew the territory. We agreed to go with him in order to have one more canoe excursion before leaving Fairbanks for the winter.

I did not mind joining up with Gustav and Elisabeth. Being with them would not "ruin" my wilderness experience. In fact I liked Gustav and his wife. I appreciated the way Gustav worked. He added order and speed to the cabin-building. Where Peter would take off half a day to drive in to town for two nails, Gustav would call together a meeting, ask everyone how many nails --- as well as other supplies --- were needed for the week, and make one trip into town to make the purchases. With Gustav on the job, we all developed a working rhythm that didn't exist before he arrived on the scene. It was balm for my soul.

Gustav had devised a plan to canoe on the Susitna, a river originating in the Alaska Mountain Range where Mt. McKinley reigns. Gustav expected a typical wilderness float trip with a few challenging white-water rapids along the way. He was unaware of the eleven-mile stretch of treacherous water along the Susitna ominously called Devil's Canyon that he would inevitably have to pass through.

Envisioning calamity on the Susitna, Peter suggested instead a

canoe trip on Birch Creek, a tributary to the Yukon River that could be reached from Steese Highway directly from Fairbanks. He said it would provide a variety of water experience and was home to interesting wildlife. Gustav knew his brother had been living in Alaska for over two years and had earned the title of "Local." Gustav figured Peter knew what he was talking about. Gustav and Elisabeth changed their plan.

But recognizing that Tobias and I were fresh from being in the wilderness, Gustav turned to us for advice on what kind of supplies he and Elisabeth should pack.

"You're planning to rent a canoe, I suppose?" I asked.

He nodded.

"Well, I wouldn't recommend getting an aluminum one. It's cold, for one thing. The cold from the water will go right through the aluminum, then right through you."

"Makes sense," he said.

"And it's loud. If it hits a rock, it makes a sound that reverberates out quite a distance. The sound gets under your skin. Plus, the reverberating sounds will scare away the animals that you're out there to see."

"Oh, we wouldn't want that," Gustav agreed.

"And another thing," I added, "it doesn't float nicely."

Gustav 's raised his right eyebrow. "So what kind does float nicely?" he asked.

"Birchbark or skin," I answered.

"I know a friend who can lease you a good canoe," Peter announced.

So Peter and Gustav started out early the next morning looking for a warm, quiet, nicely floating canoe. They were away four or five hours, going from "friend" to "friend." When they returned they were carrying a canoe...made from aluminum. It turned out that none of the friends possessed a quality canoe, and by the time Peter and Gustav reached the rental office, all the good canoes had been taken.

| 20 |

THE SECOND CANOE TRIP

While Peter and Gustav went to rent the canoe, Tobias did the laundry and Elisabeth and I drove in to town to buy food for the trip. I had done it before, so knew what and how much we needed.

Tobias and I also offered our supplies and equipment for general use so that Gustav and Elisabeth wouldn't have to buy for their separate needs. Tobias and I would sleep in my tent, and Gustav, Elisabeth and Peter would share Tobias'. Peter had to join the party because he would be guide (to show us which part of Birch Creek we should canoe), and chauffeur (his old army truck would get us to the starting point). As it turned out, the truck had no brakes.

"No problem," Peter said. "It's strong enough to take us where we need to go."

So in that army truck with no brakes, Peter, Gustav, Elisabeth, Tobias and I drove northeast for more than four hours on Steese Highway. At Peter's designated place of unloading, we bumped over some rough bushes along the side of the road in order to come to a stop, and then looked around. Where was the water? There was very little in the creek bed, and although our canoes could sit on the water, we couldn't sit in the canoes without forcing them to scrape the mud at creek bottom. Gustav and I were a bit disappointed.

Peter had another idea. "Another couple of miles ahead there's a branch where the water's wilder than you've ever seen! Why not leave the truck parked where it is and put our canoes in the stream right below the truck? We can pull our canoes to the other branch." Gray clouds hung about us and there was a steady rain. We would be walking in mountain water that was between 60 and 70 degrees Fahrenheit. Along the edge of the creek it doesn't get as cold as it gets in the water, but if Elisabeth decided to walk along the edge of the creek, it wouldn't be so warm there, either.

Why not pull the canoes to the wild water Peter promised? Why not? Were we crazy? Yes, we were. We were crazy guys from Switzerland. We attached ropes to the canoes and lowered them into the creek. We stepped into the water wearing our shoes inside our Sorel boots, and with the ropes pulled the canoes behind us in the direction Peter indicated. A person might sometimes have to pull a canoe upstream, but never downstream as we were doing now. Some parts of the creek were fifteen feet across, other parts one hundred and fifty feet. The water depth ranged from one foot to four or five feet. It was on the five-foot deep water that we played at being gondoliers. At least we could laugh at ourselves a little. As long as we managed to block out what was in and on the water.

In the water was silt. Our walking churned the water around enough so that the silt, like fine sand, easily got into our boots. When fine sand gets between the toes it becomes like sandpaper. On the water were mosquito eggs, and laying those eggs were mosquitoes that never left us alone. Sand paper between the toes and mosquitoes all around our hands and faces. This was the adventure of a lifetime.

It was a good thing that Tobias and I had already learned to adjust to the mosquitoes and their bites during our trip down the Chandalar. By the end of that trip the bites didn't itch, and I even stopped getting the red bumps. For Peter, though, the mosquitoes along Birch Creek were unbearable. He worried about bot fly larvae and warble fly larvae and slapped at himself constantly.

I found it amazing that while Peter lived in Alaska, he was still a city guy, controlled by many irritations and fears of the wild. He

hadn't used his time to gain experience in the wilderness. He never ventured out into it. He wouldn't go exploring. "I don't like to be surprised," he said.

I was in the habit of always looking ahead, looking for what would be coming up next. Tobias was being trained to do the same thing. You can be killed much more easily in the city than you can in the wilderness, by the way. Dangers in the wilderness come mostly from misjudging animals or weather, or not being prepared. In the city you can be very prepared, but the proximity of cars, construction and people moving all around you produces stress and makes safety much more of an issue.

Before I went to Alaska, people said to me, "You're crazy. You're going there just to die." But every day that I rode my motorbike to work, they could have been saying the same thing. In Zurich I very often had to deal with dangerous, even life-threatening situations. My motorbike screeched to a halt at least twice a week when car drivers, anxious to get to work, cut across me, even though I had the green go-ahead and their light showed red.

In the evenings, tired drivers failed to see me, drifted into my lane, and sidelined me. In bumper-to-bumper traffic, drivers have taken up the practice of reading-while-waiting. (Today it's cellphone-usage-while-waiting as well...) When they realize the traffic is moving, they automatically press on the gas, and many times fail to judge the distance between their vehicle and a motorbike.

Staying alert and keeping an eye out for all possibilities are crucial in the wilderness as well as in the city.

During our excursion along Birch Creek, Peter refused to go by himself to collect firewood. He often failed to sleep the whole night through because he was afraid of animals, especially bears. Once back in Fairbanks when we were building the cabin, Peter heard from a visitor that there was a bear in the area. Upon hearing that news, Peter climbed the wall of the cabin faster than I had ever seen anyone scale a wall in the army.

I myself would go looking for bears, because I trusted that unprovoked, wild bears would not attack humans. I believed that a bear might attack if he felt cornered, or if a human got too close

to him. But I knew from experience that some animals will even allow you to get quite close. Just as one must always be willing and able to read a glacier in order to enter its space and survive, one must also be willing to read an animal's behavior, and back away when necessary, in order to survive. You must sense when the animal feels threatened. What I believed was true for "animals" I believed was also true for bears. Plus, if there was ever any real danger, I had my whistle.

One of the pleasures of a canoe trip is to see the wildlife. That's one of the purposes for being in the wilderness in the first place. In order to see the animals, you have to always be on the lookout. You have to always be aware. Peter was afraid to be in the wilderness, even though he was with the rest of us. He always pulled back; he was not curious about finding what was around the next corner.

He also didn't wear the proper clothing. He brought a down jacket, even though it was summer and the weather was quite warm --- sixty to seventy degrees during the day, twenty degrees cooler at night. Too warm for down. He also brought a down hat. Peter had lived in Alaska for two years already, and still did not know how to dress for it. On this trip he wore sneakers, instead of sturdy boots.

Tobias and I wore our rubber Sorel boots that were made with a fabric inside that kept the feet warm and dry. Until you stepped right into the creek with these boots on, that is. Afterward they took quite a long time to dry. We rested them on sticks above the fire and left them drying all night.

The one thing that Peter did enjoy along with the rest of us was fishing, and eating what we caught for dinner. Tobias and I had developed a delicious recipe for roasted fish, which we very willingly shared. There are just a few easy steps:

1. Catch a fish.

2. Wrap the fresh fish in birch leaves (flat, broad leaves that bend, fold and enclose well the body of a fish).

3. Place the wrap over hot coals.

4. Watch for leaves to turn brown, then black.

5. After approximately one-half hour, scrape away blackened

leaves.

6. Serve with sour dough bread, salad greens picked from the surrounding grasses, and pine needle tea, made by pouring hot water over needles from the branch of a pine tree.

7. Enjoy a very tasty meal.

During our long watery march, Tobias remained stoic in temperament and silent in voice. There was no, "Hey, this is fun!" or "Hey, this is a really shitty trip."

If Gustav was disappointed that at that moment we weren't cruising through white water on the glacial stream of the Susitna River, he didn't show it. What a different kind of experience that would have been. Every now and then he'd look around and ask me, "Do you see anything?" If he couldn't be enjoying the thrill of the water, at least he could be enjoying the thrill of stalking a wild animal. But I saw nothing. There was no wildlife to observe. On the other hand, Elisabeth passed her time walking along the banks of Birch Creek humming to herself. She was quite pleased that she and Gustav hadn't gone down the Susitna, because she was afraid of it. "Swimming in white water is not my idea of fun," she had said when Gustav first mentioned the Susitna. "It's like swimming in a washing machine," she added without laughing. Nevertheless, she would have gone along with Gustav. Maybe being crazy was just a part of being Swiss. Maybe choosing to put ourselves into life-threatening situations when they just as easily could be avoided was just in our blood.

After three days of walking and gondoliering in and along Birch Creek, we did not find the "water wilder than you've ever seen!" that Peter promised. So Peter hitchhiked a ride back to the truck, came to pick us up, and then we drove to the Chatanika River. For two days more we canoed. Our vistas were tall pines and thick bushes, but no deer, moose, caribou, bear, or even any types of wolves or fox crossed our pathway. Then the trip ended, because Gustav's and Elisabeth's free time had ended.

They had announced when they first arrived in Alaska that they had reservations to stay on Kodiak Island and the Katmai Preserve near Anchorage in order to get a close-up view of the biggest brown bears in the world.

"How about if you come there with us?" Gustav offered.

Fabienne declined because she had to look after Petra.

I was interested in seeing the bears, but just not at that time. Going to Kodiak Island was for Gustav and Elisabeth. It was their adventure, not mine nor Tobias'. But Peter agreed to join his brother and Elisabeth. So the day after we returned from our canoe trip, Peter, Gustav and Elisabeth left for Kodiak, and for the next five days Tobias and I worked on the log cabin by ourselves.

It left me time to reflect on our first trip on the Chandalar River, and this second one along Birch Creek and the Chatanika. Two trips that were so similar in function yet so different in character and spirit. Along the Chandalar the daytime temperatures wavered between seventy-five and eighty-five degrees. We saw bears (from a distance), caribou, moose, arctic fox and that stately lynx. It was a satisfying trip, even though our route had kept us nearer to civilization than we desired. We had seen too many human beings. On our first trip I was actually disappointed that we had arrived at the Yukon Bridge so quickly. I expected the trip to last at least six weeks, but there we were, hauling in our canoe after three. My belly churned with regret. I regretted that I hadn't found a cheaper way to get to the upper regions of the Koyukuk River for our first canoe trip. I was sure the Koyukuk would have kept us out in the wild for a much longer time.

And now there was this second trip with Peter and Gustav and Elisabeth in which white water rafting was promised, but not supplied. I had hoped to see Tobias excel in the sport he knew. I had hoped to learn something new about him. I had hoped to see him, for once, take control because he was the expert. But Birch Creek was a lost opportunity.

Well, not totally, because I did learn something about myself that I think could be true for others, too. I learned that if you have a dream, it is best to follow through as soon as you can. A hope unfulfilled makes the heart sick. My heart was sick, and I knew I had to get away. I had to get away to Alaska.

And I also learned a very important piece of information. What I learned was that every person's experience with the place that is Alaska will be different.

| 21 |

PREPARING FOR WINTER

2 Swiss Guys. Would Like to Spend Winter in Wilderness. Seeking Cabin to Rent in Mountains.

A lady named Roberta Chase called us on Peter's phone, answering our newspaper ad.

"I know the precise cabin you're looking for," she said. "It's up north in the Ray Mountains, a very nice distance from Fairbanks." The Ray Mountains sit to the south and west of Arctic Village and Venetie, approximately one hundred and forty miles northwest of Fairbanks. They rise up at their tallest to an elevation of about one thousand six hundred eighty meters (or about five thousand feet "in American").

Asked if she had ever been to the cabin, Roberta answered, "No, but I have pictures of it, and the phone number of the owner, Mr. Robert Agen."

When we called Mr. Agen, he described his self-built log cabin nestled on a large plot of land he had bought in the most eastern ridge of the Ray Mountains. The mountain ridge, he explained, was bordered on the east by the Yukon River, on the south by the Tozitna River, and offered a valuable hot spring which flowed near his cabin. For almost three years Mr. Agen had remained on the Ray Mountains land with his wife and daughter.

"Would you be willing to rent your place for the winter?" we asked.

"No way," he said. "I don't know you guys. I don't know if you have any experience in the wilderness, either. And I wouldn't like the idea of finding two dead bodies in my place come springtime."

I relayed a little of what my wilderness experience had been, and the call ended.

A few days later the cabin owner phoned back saying he had had time to think and was partial to the idea of "having someone check on the cabins. See if they're okay. Look after them for a while."

I originally thought that it was only one cabin we were talking about, but in fact, there were three. Of course we only wanted to rent one, and Robert Agen, the owner, would charge us $1,000 to rent one cabin for seven months. He also asked that we wire him a $3,000 security deposit for him to use if we destroyed the cabin, or in case he had to visit the Ray Mountains himself at the end of the winter and rescue us. My mother wired the $3000 deposit from my reserve account in Switzerland. After Robert sent a map with the exact location of his cabins marked on it, and after I had wired the rental money and security deposit, I learned that it had been five years since the Agen family had lived in the Ray Mountains. The daughter had gotten sick and the weather was so bad they couldn't bring her out. She had died there.

News of a child's death in one of the cabins I'd be renting did not scare me away. I was very sorry to hear Robert Agen's sad family history, but figured something clearly had gone wrong, and perhaps he just hadn't prepared well.

Tobias and I would be well-prepared.

My real concern was the physical decline that could befall a cabin in five years. I considered what could go wrong in such an amount of time and set about gathering supplies.

The first order of business was to buy a common size stove pipe, big enough to fit over an older one, if need be, in case the stove pipe in the cabin had rusted out. A good stovepipe would be essential for cooking.

The next purchase was a fire damper, necessary to direct the smoke out of the cabin.

New door hinges were on my list, as well as a roll of thick construction plastic.

I also knew I'd be taking my tools which included the small Swiss knife, a Leatherman multi-purpose pocket tool bought in Anchorage, a buck knife, a saw, a hammer and an axe.

The task of gathering together a food supply that we'd carry with us into the winter became a weekly responsibility. During our time in Fairbanks we harvested high bush and low bush cranberries, blueberries and blackberries. Some days we went picking together, other days we went alone.

One morning I drove alone in Peter's truck north on Steese Highway until I found a beckoning cluster of blackberries. After parking the car and grabbing a large bucket suitable for gathering berries, I wandered through knee-high grass and low shrubs to a large, low patch of black fruit. The blackberries weren't just big, they were ripe, juicy and very sweet. I decided to do a little picking and a little eating at the same time. With the bucket almost full I turned to go back to the truck when one of the prickly shrubs snagged my jacket. As I reached around to extricate the jacket's sleeve from the bramble, something dark, brown, and looking awfully furry at the other end of the bushes suddenly appeared. My vision narrowed, and it was as if I were in a tunnel. I could no longer see the sky nor my jacket nor the berry bush nearby. All I could see was the bear, very much in focus, at that very moment slurping on juicy berries just as I had been doing seconds before. Mr. Bear was very close --- maybe about fifty feet away --- but up until now had not seen me. So close, so close, my mind whispered. But no other thought came. I just stood there, motionless. Then, into the tunnel a thought floated. When it sees me, will it feel cornered? And then another thought. What about the whistle? Reach into your zippered jacket and take out that long sleek piece of smooth silver so you can scare this bear away with a loud whistle!

Now I have to tell you that I very much would have liked to take out my whistle and use it, but I WAS FROZEN IN PLACE. I

couldn't move. And the bear looked up.

In what seemed like many long minutes my tunnel vision widened and my mind told me that I should really try to position something --- a rock, a shrub bigger than the berry bushes, anything --- between me and this huge sack of fur that probably weighed well over a thousand pounds. Inexplicably at that moment I considered the expression, "That guy must weigh a ton!" Anyone who says that about a person hasn't seen a fully-grown brown bear, I thought. No human being could be as big as this bear. I pictured myself laughing, and then I laughed out loud. Immediately my mind went into command mode. Move! Put something between you and the bear!

But there was nothing nearby to hide behind or place between me and the bear's imposing presence so that he wouldn't feel threatened, or so that I might feel just a little bit safer. The bear took a step toward me. In the next second my bucket was on the ground and I was doing jumping jacks. I waved my arms wildly and jumped for the sky. At the same time I shouted and grunted like a maniac. I jumped and shouted with all my might. Finally the bear lifted his huge snout into the air, gave the crazy person in front of him one last look, and turned and plodded away.

I guess I showed him who was boss.

After many long minutes of waiting until my heart rate returned to normal, I gathered up the spilled berries and stumbled back to the truck. Huh, I thought. Had I wasted money on the whistle?

Once we collected each batch of berries, Tobias and I cooked them with a small amount of sugar and made them into jams for the winter. They would provide good sources of vitamin C.

We didn't plan to leave for the mountains until the first good snowfall. With a thrill in our bones we had decided to go in by foot, or rather, by dogsled. We would rent a dog team and pack all of our supplies on the sled.

But there was one problem. The Indians from whom we wanted to rent the dogs told us it was no use. There wouldn't be enough snow on the north side of the Ray Mountains, where our cabin was located, even if we waited until October. The ground toward

the place we intended to go was hard-packed and windswept, not a conducive groundcover for sledding.

Lack of snow spoiled a romantic dream of traveling around Alaska with a pack of dogs. I had always thought that, in Alaska, snow would be plentiful, all winter long.

After the Indians nixed our plan, we had to find another way to reach the cabin.

Tobias and I each had allotted 10,000 Swiss Francs ($5,000) for our Alaskan experience. Since we each had already spent 4,000 Swiss Francs ($2,000) on the open-ended flight from Zurich to Anchorage, 900 ($450) each for the canoe, 1,000 ($500) each on the cabin rental, and 500 ($250) each on incidentals thus far, about 3,600 Swiss Francs ($1,800) each were left for us to live on for the rest of our stay. We had to closely manage our intra-Alaska travel expenses. (My mother had wired the $3,000 cabin deposit directly from my personal account in Switzerland, hopefully to be returned to that same account at the end of our stay.)

Our first option to get to the Ray Mountains was to hire a pontoon plane and pilot. If that option was chosen, we'd have to find a lake near our cabin to land on, deposit all supplies, then little by little transport the supplies from the lake to the cabin. The map indicated that the nearest lake was about ten miles from Robert Agen's cabins.

The second option was to fly in on a plane with skis, but for this option we'd have to wait much longer for more snow. After considering this second option for a short while we learned from experienced pilots that the conditions in the mountains had to be perfect for a ski plane to land. If they weren't, we'd have to turn around and come back, and still pay for the excursion. We nixed the ski plane idea.

The third option was to proceed by helicopter, which would be much more expensive than going by plane, but much more certain, and it was the only realistic option left. So we drove on over to the airport to check on prices and see if a helicopter pilot was available for hire. An Indian employee at the airport asked where we wanted to go.

"We Indians would never go to the north side of the Ray Mountains," he said. "There are bad spirits there." He coughed. "It's a spooky valley and a spooky place."

Foolishly or no, I welcomed any new experience. "I'm looking forward to it," I answered him.

※

Rob was a young and inexperienced helicopter pilot who told Tobias and me that he could not carry us plus our equipment in his helicopter at the same time. Nor would he have enough kerosene to make the trip there and back on only one tank of fuel. He proposed flying one of us in first with half the supplies, then coming back and picking up the other with the remainder of the supplies and more kerosene.

Accepting his proposal meant that, on the night before the helicopter ride, I would have to drive Tobias to a certain place on the Dalton Highway where he agreed to stay with a portion of our supplies and a barrel of oil. The road would be wide enough for a helicopter to land, and the location would be easy to locate from the air.

So on the third Friday of September I met Rob at the airport. The sky was a soupy gray. Rob wasn't sure we should make the trip. I thought about Tobias, hunkered down and waiting on that lonely spot of highway where I had dropped him off the night before, and suggested that we try.

Poor Rob had to fly in clouds most of the way and had no idea where he was going. He should have used his instruments, but they didn't seem to be working. He kept saying, "We'll be all right." But we weren't all right. He didn't even have a map. How could he know where he was going?

About an hour into the flight Rob announced, "Now we're flying along the mountain range." But I was confused. The Ray Mountains were at a much higher altitude than we had reached during the past hour of flight time. Where were we? Rob dropped the helicopter through the clouds and came upon...the Yukon River! We weren't anywhere near the mountain range. We were way too far south. Rob hadn't a clue.

Rob was forced to turn around. He flew along the Dalton Highway behind trucks and other large vehicles to guide his way back to Fairbanks. I was angry over his ignorance, and worried about fuel. Had Tobias and I just wasted close to 1,500 Swiss francs each on this flight?

Success on any such adventure requires wise decision-making, and I had just made an unwise decision.

Luckily the owner of the helicopter company gave us a partial refund, but only partial because he said I had given the go ahead for the trip even though visibility was very poor.

✳

Tobias and I began to consider other winter places that we could reach without using a helicopter:

We could go down to the lake in Anchorage where the lady offered us a cabin. (Too many people around and too much of a chance for snowmobilers.)

A house on a ridge near Fairbanks, where no one lived close by. (It was wilderness, but not wilderness enough, and there were no mountains.)

We were offered a job at a gold mine, which we could reach by car. The mine was east of the Brooks Range, which is the most northern mountain range in Alaska. The one disadvantage of this location is that it wasn't a place to do the mountaineering trips I hoped to do. The job was to monitor the mine to prevent theft of the miners' gear that they left during the winter. Our presence would help ensure that their gear would still be available when they returned the following summer. This wasn't what I wanted to experience. Gold mines were dark and dreary places, where nature was being torn apart. I wanted to be where nature was intact, and no other human frequented. The sleeping arrangements at the gold mines were cold and uncomfortable boxcars from trains, meant to be used only in the summer. All of the food we needed would have already been stored there, so the experience of subsisting off the land would have been denied. It was true that we would have earned money living near a gold mine, but I didn't want to be responsible for warding off thieves.

Tobias and I talked it over. Or rather, as usual, I talked and Tobias listened and nodded. Would it be worth the additional money to take a helicopter a second time? Could Jim, the owner of the helicopter company that employed young Rob who tried to transport us the first time, be convinced to fly us in again for less money? Couldn't hurt to ask. Jim had an opening during the second week of October, and on that day he assured us he would be our pilot.

| 22 |

EARLY DAYS IN
THE MOUNTAINS

The Yukon River Dalton Bridge is approximately eighty miles from Fairbanks, and by the second week of October, the highway to the bridge was covered with solid snow. It took Tobias and me almost four hours to drive there. I helped Tobias unload his supplies and set up his tent. Below the bridge, the Yukon River had already started to freeze. A strong wind was blowing from the north. All signs were pointing to one cold night for Tobias. But he was his usual stoic self. "Don't let Jim forget that I'm here," was all he said when I waved goodbye.

The next morning was beautiful and clear, with a temperature of -10°F. I wore long underwear, woolen trousers, a long sleeve cotton shirt beneath a wool sweater and a wool lumberjack jacket. Jim had on insulated overalls and a long-sleeve wool shirt. The helicopter engine, I knew, would provide some heat inside the cockpit.

"Glad for the cold," Jim said with a smile as he helped me load my supplies into the copter. "This amount of weight might have been a problem in warmer weather." I knew from my army days that cold air is more compact, and therefore heavier than warmer air, which means that it can carry more weight.

As I settled into my seat, Jim handed me a map, placed one across his lap, and started the engine. Slowly the helicopter lifted to about six feet above the ground. Seeing that the weight was

manageable, Jim landed the helicopter again and put in ten more gallons of fuel. We originally had plans to go up to the Yukon Bridge and fill up the tank once more, but now that wouldn't be necessary.

As we lifted off the second time, I saw in the distance to the south of us majestic Mount McKinley, North America's highest mountain peak. Jim righted the helicopter and headed north. We were on our way.

Jim was always careful to crosscheck where I pinpointed our location on my map with where he pinpointed our location on his. It took us more than two hours to reach the Ray Mountains. I saw the range's craggy peaks from quite far away.

"There they are," I said out loud, more than once.

The helicopter climbed up very close to the south side of the eastern ridge. We came over the top, and below were the valley and the woods that I recognized from Robert Agen's map. And there, THERE, were the cabins. They were four actually: an octagonal cabin, a rectangular cabin, a tiny shack high up on the mountainside, and further down the mountain, about a half a mile from the others, sat the cabin we rented for the winter.

Jim was controlling the helicopter, but it was as if --- rising up, up, up, and then peeking over the Ray Mountains into the valley below --- I was the one who was flying. I felt like a bird entering a brand new country. My chest expanded and I was overwhelmed with excitement. All of my senses were awakening, one by one.

After landing outside the forest on snow-covered tundra, about a thousand feet from the bottom cabin, we unloaded all of the supplies. Jim gave me a hug, jumped back into the helicopter and with it raised himself high above me. He hung over the upper cabins for a few moments so that I could orient myself, and then took off.

As the helicopter disappeared into the cerulean sky, the engine noise faded away, leaving neither a speck nor a cloud in that great dome all about me. Everything --- the vibrant blue above, the crystal white below, the fringes of evergreen in between --- everything at that moment was very still. No rustling tree nor

wind nor animal cry could be heard. All was calm. All was bright.

In my diary afterward I wrote that this was a most beautiful time of silence, a moment I had yearned for, for such a long, long time.

Finally I picked up my backpack and Tobias' rifle, and began a zigzag search through the woods, looking for the lower cabin we had seen from the air. The growth of trees and bushes hid it quite well. I could almost touch it before I saw it.

The door was ajar, so I stepped inside, bypassing snow and animal droppings. Light from the doorway revealed how perfectly ample the fourteen feet by fourteen feet cabin was, and feeling immediately at home, I shut the door. Wood shutters hung loosely over the windows, preventing adequate light from entering, so I moved to open the door right away, and just enough light revealed a beautiful painting on the door's interior side. The painting consisted of three very finely drawn circles surrounded by a wreath of green leaves. The center circle held a mustard-colored cross on a blue-gray hill and a woman with long, dark hair at the bottom of the hill raising her arms to the cross. The left circle contained a graphic golden sun with rays projecting outward, and in between the rays a line drawing of what looked like a buttery yellow bird with two large eyes flying right toward the vibrant daystar. The right circle contained a portion of cobalt blue, with a crescent moon inside the blue, and outside the portion of blue the remaining area of the circle was painted black, as if it were outer space surrounding a blue earth.

I tried to understand right then what the painting meant, but recognized there'd be plenty of time to think about it later. However, what captured me in the moment was the novelty of such a refined piece of art existing in such a crude, isolated cabin. Out in the middle of nowhere, on the back of a roughly sanded door, there was evidence that a living, breathing soul had previously resided here. It occurred to me then that it could be a sign. But I'd think about that later, too.

Better bring the supplies in before something freezes unexpectedly and cracks, I thought. But when I tugged on the leather strap to go back outside, the door wouldn't open. I was a

prisoner!

After studying the leather pull on the inside of the door more closely, it struck me: the door had been improperly constructed. Normally cabin doors aren't made to open to the inside. Animals can lean on them and fall right in, inviting destruction to follow after.

If I keep pulling on the leather handle, I'll pull it right off and never be able to get out at all. I felt around in my pocket and breathed a sigh of relief when I found my Swiss army knife there. Using it to dig into the jam, I forced a slight separation. Then with more digging and tugging I finally wedged my fingers in between the jam and the door and jerked the door ajar.

With the door open again I examined the cabin more critically and saw that the stovepipe had indeed rusted away. That would need replacing. The plastic sheeting over the windows would need to be changed, and something had to be done about the sticking door. Other than those few things, a little clean up and clean out and the cabin would be livable. I was satisfied.

The surrounding area of the cabin offered a river close by and a handsome view down valley. Outside, I walked larger and larger circles around the cabin to survey the surrounding woods, returned to the supply drop, and began carrying the most fragile things back to the cabin. It was quite a job bringing the bags and tools through the bushes. The whole process made me glad we had chosen the helicopter method of transport instead of using an airplane. The helicopter supply drop was much closer to the cabin than where a pontoon plane could have landed. Moving our supplies from ten miles away would have taken us a week or more.

I placed the rifle in the far corner of the cabin, out of the way. Tobias bought the rifle, and I agreed to bring it to the mountains in case our cabin burned down and all of our food and other belongings were destroyed. If those things happened, the gun would be needed to hunt for food.

In fact, Tobias and I had made a pact that if we found Robert Agen's cabin already burnt or fallen apart, we would build a new one. We had our tools.

I pulled two petroleum lamps from my rubber sack and set them on the small wooden kitchen table. These would be our defense against Arctic winter darkness, but needed to be used with caution. If one of those lamps got filled up too much with oil while it was still warm, it could explode. A log cabin would catch fire very easily after such an explosion. But I knew that wouldn't be the most dangerous part of the disaster. The most dangerous part in winter would be the destruction of all extra clothing and food. Death comes, then, from overexposure to the elements, and from starvation. Hence, Tobias' desire for the gun.

In Fairbanks we learned that a lot of people die in the wilderness because their cabins burn down, and they have no cache. A cache is a fancy word for a platform raised above ground so that animals cannot reach it. A simple cache structure might use four tall, sturdy tree trunks that are dug into the ground like fence posts, but equidistant apart. A platform of logs or plank wood is tied to the trunks at least ten to twelve feet above the ground. A ladder is used to reach the platform.

So without a cache, those whose cabin is destroyed end up freezing or starving to death.

I went back outside to look around carefully for Robert Agen's cache. But in the distance there was the sound of the helicopter, so I ran to the open and waved my arms.

"It was a nice flight out here to the Ray Mountains," Tobias announced when Jim dropped him down from the sky. "Have you found the cabin already?"

"Yep, and it's still standing," I answered. I asked Jim if he wanted to have a nice cup of hot coffee before heading back.

"Sure would like to get back to Fairbanks by sundown," he said, "and I've got to stop and refuel at the Yukon Bridge because I'm running low. Thanks, though. Maybe next time..."

We unloaded the second half of our supplies quickly and gave our thanks to a very solid pilot.

"I wish you good luck," Jim said. "It gets damn cold out here."

After I helped Tobias with the transfer of supplies, he and I went exploring. We found the nearby cache built for our cabin

and climbed the ladder to check out what Robert Agen had stored there. The food, clothes and blankets on top of the platform were covered in sailcloth that was tied down with rope. Most of the food was too old to be usable, but the structure would still work as our cache. So after wrapping our extra food and clothing in a thick blanket, we placed it under the sailcloth. We planned to take down a week's supply of food at a time.

The hot spring that fed the river near our cabin originated further up the mountain near the main cabins and maintained a temperature of about 100 degrees Fahrenheit. I figured Mr. Agen had built the cabins in this location because he intended to put that hot spring to use, although we didn't see any piping. We considered using the spring for bathing, but the question was, how to get from the spring back to the cabin without freezing to death? The water would ice over on our bodies immediately. I did notice that there was a bucket in the cabin (I had brought a collapsible one in case we didn't find another one) and was satisfied that at least after transporting warm water into the cabin, we could take sponge baths.

Our outhouse was a simple hole in the ground. After the first storm, though, we built an igloo around the hole to keep us a little warmer as we performed our bodily functions. It worked quite well, keeping out all the wind and a lot of the cold.

On the first day at our mountain retreat we installed the new stovepipe, put plastic sheeting in the windows so the wind wouldn't whistle through the cabin, and swept out the animal droppings and other natural debris with a couple of tree branches.

The temperature inside the cabin that first day hovered around 35°F. That first night we got to bed quite late because of all the work we had to do. I did have a watch with me and was comforted that the cold did not stop it from working.

We awoke at nine the next morning. The temperature was 28°F inside the cabin. Outside the cabin it was a brisk -11°F.

We decided not to heat the cabin above 38 degrees Fahrenheit, understanding that the body is subjected to a huge shock if it is passes from a much warmer temperature inside to anywhere from -11°F to -50°F outside a couple of times a day. Inside we wore

woolen socks, woolen trousers and cotton shirts with woolen pullovers, and felt very comfortable.

My plan for the first two weeks:

1. Gather and chop easy-access wood.

We used the wood from dead trees nearby, and then stacked it right next to the outside walls of the cabin. Stacking the logs around the outside of the cabin served the purpose of insulating the cabin for us as well.

2. Grind grain for baking bread.

We stored the grain in plastic food containers with closed lids that a food store in Fairbanks was only going to throw away. We knew there was a chance of the plastic becoming brittle and breaking, so we made sure we brought extra containers with us.

The iron pot we brought with us would be used to make bread that could last for two days.

3. Restock dwindling woodpile.

The job of finding firewood became more arduous as the circle of used up deadwood around the cabin increased. It took us about two weeks to consume all of the dead timber close by, so we found ourselves having to go farther and farther away to keep our supply well-stocked.

Nevertheless, searching for firewood became a pleasant daily task for me. During the first few weeks several choruses of Ruffed Grouse --- well-feathered medium-sized birds sometimes called partridges in other parts of the world --- piqued my curiosity. In winter, the toes of these chestnut-to-white-feathered birds (with chocolate-colored feathers around the neck) grow projections from their sides that resemble tiny combs. Ruffed Grouse are ground lovers, and these projections help them snowshoe across the ground's white mantle! They also stay warm and confuse their predators by burying themselves down long snow burrows. It can be -30°F outside but rarely colder than +20°F underneath the snow.

Sometimes I would walk out at night and be surprised by a Ruffed Grouse as it burst through the dome of his burrow like an exploding chestnut feather ball, either thinking it would scare me,

or was startled by my movement. White Snowshoe Hares, some almost two feet long with exceptionally large furry feet and long ears, would scatter in the light of the moon on top of hardened snowdrifts because of the Grouse explosions.

The Willow Ptarmigan were frequent and abundant guests to my backyard. Resembling small grouse except for their thickly-feathered toes and white wings, they often made me laugh out loud as they sat quietly on the snow, thinking I couldn't see them. Knowing that this was their nature was comforting because I figured that if ever Tobias and I got hungry, we could set snares and catch the ptarmigan easily.

But I felt pretty confident we would have enough to eat on a vegetarian diet. We brought with us dried green beans, yellow peas, lentils, soybeans, kidney and garbanzo beans, millet, barley, corn, spaghetti, rice, wheat, oats, dried fruits, and nuts. We allotted ourselves three pieces of fruit a day from the supply of dried pineapples, apples, and pears purchased in a grocery store in Fairbanks. Oatmeal every morning for breakfast was a must. I always mixed up milk powder with water to pour over the oats, but Tobias ate his dry.

We were using a lot of body energy to stay warm. I wouldn't recommend living in the wilderness to lose weight, but it's an effective method. All the extra fat on my body was slowly melting away. Of course I didn't eat as much as I was used to eating in Switzerland, but I continued to feel strong and energetic. All of our food in the mountains was high-quality and natural. Whether working or hiking, my body maintained its durability.

Freshly made muffins and cookies were everyday treats that provided energy, with each of us trying to come up with a different recipe every few batches. We had brought a muffin form with us, and baked muffins in it on top of the stove. The combination of the muffin tin on top of the stove with the iron skillet turned upside down over it worked like an oven.

We saved the dried beans for special occasions.

I didn't have a calendar. Only in my diary did I have a record of the days, and then the months, that passed by. Tobias also kept a diary, which I never read, even though I was curious. He left it

open several times on the table, and I was sorely tempted to read the thoughts of someone who spoke so little to me, who offered so very little of himself. But I never gave in to that temptation.

Completing the tasks necessary for daily life in the wilderness in winter takes quite a while: chopping wood, transporting it to the cabin, grinding grain, baking, preparing the water, cooking the food. I was busy during those first few weeks in the mountains, and never once saw any warning pictures.

| 23 |

PRIMAL FEAR

Sometimes the temperature inside the cabin at night fell to as low as 5°F. In the morning Tobias and I bargained with each other for the right to stay in the warmth of the sleeping bag while the other one got up to start the fire. It became a game.

"You go today and I'll do it tomorrow," Tobias would say.

"But you're closer to the stove right now," I'd answer.

"And you always have a brilliant fire in less than five minutes," Tobias would counter. Tobias always thought he had great bargaining power with that bit of flattery. But it never bothered me that Tobias took longer to build the fire. Lingering in my sleeping bag gave me more time for deep breathing and reflection. Between the sleeping bag and the raised wooden platform upon which our sleeping bags lay, we positioned some air mattresses. They provided insulation from the cold ground and offered comfortable bedding.

Once the fire was built, we dressed quickly, hung our air mattresses above the stove fire to defrost, drew water from the stream, washed, made our coffee, ate, talked about what we would do for the day, replaced the used kindling and firewood at the stove, and set off.

The first bits of local scenery we inspected were the other cabins on the property. The main cabin was filled with all the essentials of a typical furnished house: mattresses, blankets, dishes, pots

and pans. The added attractions were two ski-doos, parked right inside the front door. We climbed the cache to see what was stored there, and found food enough for ten years. Unfortunately it was all stale and inedible, like the food in the other cache.

The smallest cabin held a library, which became my source of entertainment for the many stormy days and nights that filled our calendar. I kept track of time using my watch, which had dials showing the month and the day. The watch never faltered.

Of course we wanted to explore the valley all around us, and were curious about what lay on the other side of the hills to the north.

Our first hike started out as a walk, and I dressed in what I thought would provide adequate comfort and warmth: my regular cotton underwear, a long-sleeve cotton shirt, wool pullover, mountaineering trousers, my lumberjack jacket, a pair of Sorel boots, a woolen cap and gloves.

When you enter a new territory, you concentrate on having all of your senses open. After a while, you get lulled into thinking everything will stay the same and you no longer have to pay attention to the details. Tobias and I had already been in the Ray Mountains for two weeks and felt comfortable with our surroundings. We trusted them. We thought we knew them. So we went out for a little walk without thinking. Our defenses were down and we allowed ourselves to do what no wilderness hiker should ever do. We carried with us no backpack, no water, and no survival gear around our waists. We thought we were going out for a "look-see." We would be around our "home." No worries. We had on the clothes and boots we would wear for hiking in the mountains in Switzerland, but nothing special for sub-freezing temperatures near the Arctic Circle. As we started out I carried with me that long-held feeling of invincibility.

We wandered along further and further away from our cabin as people who are looking for seashells might stroll along a seashore, not so much paying attention to where we were going, but rather looking at what was right in front of us. The further we went, the more unaware we were of how far we had actually gone. Time seemed irrelevant until small gusts of wind reminded me to check

my watch. I saw we had been walking for almost five hours.

The gusts increased in intensity and very quickly shook loose from the ground a million tiny pellets of hardened snow and swirled them around us. It felt like being suddenly caught in the middle of a dust storm. White crystals sanded our faces. Tobias wore the same kind of gear I did. We appeared to be twins. Just the color of our coats was different. And we both felt the bite of the storm. It took no time at all for the cold to twist its tendrils up and into my jacket. I swore to myself that I would never wear such a jacket out into these mountains again. I hugged my arms to my chest. Tobias followed me in a silent march back to the cabin. We didn't want to waste our breath on speaking. At least I didn't. In those return-to-cabin hours I was experiencing something I didn't recognize. Normally I don't feel the icy chill of winter. Normally it will not dig into me like it does other people. But on that day I became chilled to the bone. Nothing I did worked to warm me. I could not will it, and walking faster could not produce it. If I walked faster, gritty snow bombarded my eyes with such velocity that I thought I might be blinded. So I was forced to walk backwards. Again, Tobias mimicked me. I was being controlled by an outside force, and felt out of control. An unrecognizable emotion overwhelmed me and I began to shake inside, become disoriented, and mentally go dark.

I remembered the storm with Ursula and Reguli from childhood, and stoically marched on, using the memory of that time as proof that we would make it back to the cabin without losing any fingers or toes. It was imperative that I inwardly convince myself that we would make it back. Tobias' steady step behind me was a type of encouragement. It never waivered, and he never complained.

At last we saw the pathway to the cabin, and quickly followed it to the front door.

Our habit when we entered the cabin was to take off our boots, which we kept inside so they wouldn't freeze, and nudge our feet into soft down boots brought from Switzerland. Then we removed our backpacks with the snow shoes attached, and one of us would start the fire. It is an unspoken rule that, in every wilderness cabin, firewood and kindling should always be chopped and

instantly available to start a fire. Every day upon departing the cabin Tobias and I made sure that there was a stack of wood and enough kindling for immediate use upon our return. After a warm fire was aglow, someone had to bring in drinking water from the stream. We were lucky that the stream near the cabin was close to the hot spring source, which required a simple walk outside to fill up our bucket with the liquid. Only below the cabin did the stream start to freeze up.

Next we'd decide what to cook for dinner, and two hours later sit down to eat.

On this night after the walk in frozen hell led to exhaustion, we lingered around the fire much longer than normal before completing the rest of the tasks. I stared into the flames, intertwining my fingers, wiggling my toes, and touching my ears and nose again and again to make sure there was still sensation in every extremity.

That night as I lay in my sleeping bag, I marveled at this new emotion that had attached itself to me hours before. I acknowledged that the emotion was fear. I took fear out and looked at it first from one angle and then another. I had never been so cold as on this afternoon. I had begged my body to warm itself to no avail. I felt powerless. It was a strange feeling, and the feeling created a crack in my wall of invincibility.

24

LIVING INSIDE

In the cabin during the day there was need for only a few pieces of layered clothing: a cotton undershirt, a long-sleeve cotton shirt, and over the top of these two shirts a sheep wool pullover that hadn't been dry-cleaned. Not dry-cleaning the wool left the animal grease still intact, which meant that the pull-over would help my body retain its heat much more efficiently. The bottom half of the ensemble consisted of cotton long-underwear and plain wool mountaineering trousers brought from Switzerland.

At night I slept in short underwear and a round cap on my head that my mother had knitted out of alpaca wool. Staying warm in the sleeping bag was never a problem. If I needed to go to the outhouse at night, I pulled on a pair of winter flight trousers --- those light, but very warm, nylon fiber pants with a polyester insulation --- that I got from an army surplus store in Fairbanks.

One of our first housekeeping tasks was to find a way to secure, in a standing position, all the candles essential for our nighttime work. We had brought with us boxes of white, thick, eight-inch tall candles that people store in their houses to use when the electricity goes out. We found that those candles produced such a nice, fine light for reading, writing and other nighttime tasks that we decided to use our oil lamps only when absolutely necessary. The smell from the oil lamps was overwhelmingly unpleasant, and we had plenty of candles. But we needed a way to allow the candles to stand securely. I suggested to Tobias that we create

some candleholders.

Tobias had never carved anything out of wood, so he watched me as I demonstrated how to do so. From the pinewood chopped for our fireplace, I chose pieces of slender logs that were too nice to burn. We each sawed off a six inch-piece, shaved away the outer bark and made sure the bottom edge was flat. Then, taking burning ashes from the fire and setting them in a small circle on the upside flat edge of the log, we formed a hole in the log. After the ashes burned a circular hole into the wood, we carved a little further down, allowing us to set a candle firmly inside. Tobias worked on his knife skills by creating more of these candleholders, and we soon had enough standing candles to provide good light for all nighttime activities.

During the evenings my cabin-mate and I also shared the work of grinding grain. Robert Agen had told us there would be a grain grinder in the cabin, and we found it in good condition in one of the wall cabinets. If we hadn't found it, we would have used stones to grind our grains into flour.

Every night I entered the day's observations in my diary. Tobias followed that practice as well. I used a mechanical pencil with refillable lead, so there was never any fear of running out of a sharpened writing tool.

Twice a week we transported water from the hot spring to wash clothes and give ourselves sponge baths. Tobias' feet had a tendency to smell, so he submitted them to water therapy in order to correct his body chemistry and get rid of the smell. Every few days he'd slip out of the cabin for a walk in the stream with naked feet. Sadly for both of us, the therapy didn't work.

Tobias never got bored. He was just as interested as I was in the world that surrounded us. And he worked on himself as a person quite a bit. He was ready and willing to take charge of his own experience.

He never complained. He would watch how I did things, and then try to do them on his own. He understood what the most important things to be done were, and did them.

That impressed me a lot. Not a lot of people would do what

Tobias did. Others might be afraid of the silence, or afraid of the cold, or afraid of the danger. So many of the people I knew thought I was crazy, and thought that what we were doing was very dangerous, too dangerous an adventure for a normal person.

Tobias began going off into the wilderness for increasingly longer periods of time. I never thought he would get lost. After our first "walk" he made sure he was consistently prepared and never left without a backpack. In his backpack, he, like me, always included a thermos with water, dried fruit, nuts, and a down coat. We both often carried our cameras with us when we went out. I tucked mine into the pocket of my shirt. All the metal parts of the camera were covered with special cable tape so my face wouldn't burn when I put the camera up next to it to take a picture. I learned this lesson the hard way after I had burned my fingers with a metal ice pick while mountaineering in Switzerland.

In Alaska it was also necessary to take extra caution to preserve the camera's batteries. Too late I found out that if batteries get too cold, they run out of energy. So with one camera battery dead, I carefully stored the only remaining one in my sleeping bag.

During the mountain storms Tobias and I occupied ourselves carving figurines and kitchen utensils out of northern white pine and spruce wood.

Over the winter months Tobias improved his skill using a buck knife in addition to his skill with a Swiss army knife. After finishing the candle-holders, he accepted progressively more difficult assignments. I used both types of knives to carve a whale, and as a second assignment (after the candle holders), Tobias carved one, too. Then we went on to create bears, butterflies, and long kettle soup spoons.

| 25 |

SKIING

My mother is a rather short, thin person who gives the impression of being physically weak. But she has a lot of emotional strength --- strength enough to persevere in difficult circumstances and strength enough to walk long distances. From her I learned that a person can be much stronger than what he or she appears to be. And from her I learned that it is not so much a person's physical strength that leads to survival in difficult situations, but rather it is a person's psychological strength. In many situations, psychological strength can be much more helpful than physical strength.

The odd thing is that pushing yourself to the edge physically --- like running a marathon --- can actually develop mental toughness.

Which is one of the reasons that I had encouraged Tobias to train himself physically before leaving St. Gallen. I knew that in Alaska Tobias would be tested physically. Mountain climbing always presents difficult routes to conquer. Usually the most difficult parts of a "climb" are on the descent. A lot of accidents happen on the way down.

When I first met Tobias, he appeared soft and doughy from the outside. His muscles were not well-formed and he swayed in the wind. Nevertheless, I became convinced that if Tobias could survive his parents, he could survive much more. Tobias' determination to travel halfway around the world to live in a

frozen wilderness demonstrated an internal power that I hoped he could call on in order to survive whatever difficult circumstances he encountered in Alaska.

The summertime in Alaska was the test. My stipulation was that Tobias pass the summertime test. If things between us didn't work out in the summer, then I would proceed with my winter plans solo, and Tobias would be free to do what he willed.

So in the summer, as we hiked and camped and worked with an axe and a chain saw, I'm sure Tobias felt that I was watching, waiting for him to fail. More than once Peter, Fabienne and I wondered if Tobias was going to cut off an arm or a leg using the axe or the saw, but Tobias survived intact, and we both made it to the winter, to the place where we would mountaineer.

On the morning of our first mountaineering expedition I went outside to assess the landscape. See what the snow was like. Smell the weather. I had smelled snow a few days before. My nose recognizes if what's coming will be a dry snow or a wet snow. If the weather stinks, then very soon a very wet snow, almost like rain, will spill out from the heavens. If I ever smelled stinky weather up in the mountains in Switzerland, I knew I had to get down to the valley as soon as possible because this type of weather causes avalanches. Even if there aren't avalanches, the snow is so heavy that you can't move in it. Then fog appears and there's a whiteout. You won't be able to see and it's very dangerous to hike/ski/slide down a mountain if you can't see. If you fail to get down the mountain before it's too late, you have to dig a hole into the snow and stay there for two or three days, until the weather passes, and you can see again.

When I told Tobias about the varying weather smells, he began to pay attention and started smelling the differences, too. Eventually I could smell --- a day or so ahead --- when even a windstorm would strike.

In our Ray Mountain valley there was a small, four-mile wide sliver of woodland that grew on either side of the river. Further up the mountains, right above the main cabins, there were no trees. Our cabin was about two miles down from the tree line. Robert Agen had cut down the trees around where the main

cabins stood in order to build those same cabins. But that left the main homestead area with almost no wind protection. One half mile down the mountain, where our little cabin sat, the forest still grew and we were very well-protected. Plus, right by our cabin we had the river, frozen down below but fed by a natural hot spring beginning up by Robert Agen's main cabins and still warm by the time it reached our cabin. If ever we planned an outing, we always had a natural landmark to show us the way back home.

After assessing the weather on the morning set for mountaineering, I scanned the area to the southeast of us where snow covering a treeless mountain sparkled like crystal. It offered the perfect venue for our skis.

"Today we go mountaineering!" I announced to Tobias upon reentering the cabin.

The temperature outside was a brisk -13°F. In order to use our skis we would need to use cross-country ski boots, which were the only boots that would fit into the ski bindings. On a morning like this, I would have preferred to use the bunny boots, which were much, much warmer. But the boots were only a minor deterrent. We were going mountaineering!

Onto the bottoms of the cross-country skis, in place of sealskin, which we didn't have and couldn't buy in Anchorage or Fairbanks, we tied pieces of polyester rope instead. The rope was cheap and it stung in our hands as we worked with it, but at least it appeared sturdy.

Inside the cabin we poured hot tea into thermoses and packed freshly baked bread and a daily ration of nuts and dried fruit into our backpacks.

During our time in the mountains, Tobias lay upon my shoulders all of the responsibility regarding how and where we would proceed. Everything was new out there for Tobias. He watched and waited for me to act. The truth was that everything was new out there for me, too. How could I know if things would work out as I planned? Yet I expected and accepted the responsibility. I wasn't always as self-assured as Tobias thought. Maybe my plan for the day wouldn't turn out as expected. Maybe everything would go to pieces.

On this day I experienced a thrill for the excursion we would take. In fact, each venture out thus far had given me a thrill. The first time doing anything is always exciting. You see something new. You experience something unique and fresh.

When preparing for our day trips, one of us packed the bread, the other packed the nuts. After doing it a third time, it had become a habit to take what the other person hadn't picked up.

We set off through the forest on snowshoes, those things that look like tennis rackets. We needed the snowshoes to prevent us from sinking down below the top layer of snow, but wearing them made progress difficult.

It took us about an hour and a half to reach the base of our mountain, which was stacked with snow-covered boulders. We donned the skis, and climbed through the boulders as if going uphill on moguls.

We climbed up for another hour and a half, actually not as high as I would have liked. I chose this mountain because Tobias let me know that he wasn't opposed to skiing down on open terrain, creating wide, beautiful tracks. Going higher would have put us in narrower pathways and I still questioned Tobias' skill.

At the crest of a hill, I paused, not wanting to hurry anything on this clear, beautiful day.

"Let's see how it will work out from here," I suggested.

We snacked on some bread, nuts, and one piece of dried fruit each. Then we drank hot tea from the thermoses. My hands were warm in my woolen gloves, but my feet were already chilled in the cross-country ski boots I was wearing.

No matter. The work of leg bends while skiing down would warm up my feet.

We removed the rope from the skis, packed it away, bracketed our boots, and took off!

The snow, hard beneath our slats, wouldn't allow us to dig in easily. We made wide turns, and I was grateful for the space to create the arcs. After recognizing the composition of the type of ground-cover, knowing from many years of practice how I could

edge my skies into the gritty snow, I increased speed and moved ahead of Tobias. I was flying! The wind chill made the temperature a good twenty degrees colder than the thermometer read at -13° F. Okay. Maybe I should slow down a little.

Suddenly I heard a WHAP, quickly crouched low and my left ski slid down the hill ahead of me. I looked at my boot. The bindings had broken! The boot still had one piece of the binding attached to it. "What shitty stuff is this?" I asked out loud.

Tobias stopped above me when he saw what happened. As he made his way slowly toward me, both of his bindings cracked, too. He stooped down and fiddled with the metal. "Bummer" was all he said.

Apparently the temperature was just too cold for the metal bars. The bindings were not able to withstand such extreme cold and gave up from the stress.

I had already determined that those useless slats lying on the snow in front of us weren't made for climbing up a mountain. I knew from experience that with cross-country skis, bad things can happen. One of the first bad things that can happen on cross-country skis is, if you're out in the wilderness with them you very easily can get stuck in deep snow. I had had the feeling from the first that this equipment wouldn't work out --- from the time we were at the sport shop in Anchorage where there were no wide mountaineering skis to be found. They were what we needed. I should have taken my own advice and given up on the idea then.

I looked to see if we could fix the bindings, but that would take time, and already it was starting to get darker, and colder. We had to get back.

We gathered up the useless equipment and "skied" the rest of the way down using only our boots.

Tobias was disappointed; I was deflated. This had certainly not worked out as I had planned.

❄

We did take one more ski trip before the Arctic sun disappeared during the day. On that trip we used our snowshoes. We had the kind with the long tails, and they were reasonably functional as

skis. Some mountains were steep, but not as high or as steep, or as rocky, as those in the Alps. We made something out of nothing.

Daylight lessened with the passing of each twenty-four hour period, and towards the end of November, the sun showed up for only short windows of time.

| 26 |

DENTAL HYGIENE

It was the pain in my tooth that woke me. I had asked my dentist before leaving Zurich to make sure that I wouldn't have any complications with this particular tooth, explaining that I'd be gone for a year, staying in very cold weather, far from civilization.

On this particular morning I realized that the filling had fallen out and upon stepping out into the cold to retrieve the day's water, pain surged through my jaw like a nine-inch needle. The pain worsened with each passing day. My dentist had given me replacement filling for such a problem as this, but the material wouldn't stay in the tooth cavity, and I was miserable. Tobias agreed to walk back to Fairbanks with me. It was only the third week of November. We had told our friends that we would walk out sometime in the spring. They would never be looking for us so soon.

Tobias and I prepared our sleds --- those kinds of cheap plastic round sleds that kids use for fun --- with our sleeping bags, tent, gun, axe, thermoses, extra clothes, and food for about eight days. In winter it's easier to pull a sled behind you than to carry everything on your back. We secured the food we were leaving behind in the cache, and shuttered the windows. We had brought with us from Fairbanks one bottle of wine that we planned to enjoy at Christmastime. If we abandoned it in the cabin all corked up, we were sure it would freeze and the bottle would crack. So we uncorked it and stood it on the table to wait for our return. We were ready.

But the weather wasn't cooperating. A fierce storm barreled in on

us.

Sometimes from a distance I would be mesmerized by storms and the power they displayed in scattering huge mounds of snow and totally rearranging the scenery. Though it was thrilling to watch a storm from a distance, it was frightening to be in the middle of one. The noise alone that a close storm produced was ferocious, like the sound of a jet engine.

The storm that came up the night before our planned departure was not raging at a distance. It attacked us at close range. With every howl I ducked my head deeper into my sleeping bag, but that did not prevent the noise of the howling engine from reaching inside my head. The banging of a loose window shutter added to the dissonance and began to grate on my nerves. Snow bombarded the roof in waves. Whole piles of snow were thrown at our little cabin windows over and over again.

In the morning three days later, the wind finally turned to a whimper and I thought I figured out why Robert Agen had built his cabin door to open inward. He expected that storm snow could pile so high in the entryway that he'd have to dig his way out. If the door were hinged to open to the outside, he would not have been able to open it for, I don't know, maybe the whole winter?

But when I opened the door on that morning in late November, I saw that most of the snow had been blown away. Outside cabin-high drifts abounded, but no snow blocked the door.

By nine o'clock that same morning Tobias and I had finished our morning preparations and were on our way, accompanied by beautiful emerald green and sapphire blue Northern Lights. They danced on the dark dome that hung low around us, as if they were heralding the commencement of our journey. They gave me energy, and I was uplifted. My tooth was filled with the dentist's packing, and for the time being, the pain had subsided.

Then fog descended over the mountains, and we could see only a few yards in front of us. Along our trail we noticed caribou tracks and very fresh grizzly prints. The grizzly prints were a surprise because bears are usually in hibernation after the first snowfall.

For a bear to be walking about in late November meant he was sick, hurt, or hungry, all things dangerous to us. If we had a choice we would have gone far away from the prints, but they were headed in the same direction we were. We soldiered on, and so did the prints. We knew we had to continue across the mountains until we reached the forest line before we stopped for the night. With only our tent for protection, we needed the shelter of the trees. If we set up our tent exposed on the mountainside, and if snow or another storm came in the night, we could wind up dead by morning. And what about that bear?

Tobias untied the gun from the sled and grasped it securely under his right arm as he trudged on, always behind me. I kept my thoughts to myself, wondering if he could ever bring himself to use it.

Suddenly the ground vibrated. I stopped and glanced back to see Tobias raise the gun to his shoulder.

There was an explosion of noise, but not from the gun.

It was the sound of animal hooves loping over the hard-packed snow. I crouched low to the ground. A flash of white fur came into view, lingered, and I made out the form of a beautiful mountain goat. Then quickly it continued its streak past us down the rugged mountain we climbed upon. In pursuit of the goat was a lumbering brown bear. We stayed low and the bear followed after the goat, away from us.

Tobias and I walked well over thirteen hours before we reached the beginning of the forest and could decide on a camping spot. We found a sheltered area quickly and Tobias immediately started gathering firewood. I hurriedly cleared away an area of soft snow to "install" our tent. According to the manufacturer's directions I was to dig the single middle tent pole into the ground. I did. But it was when I attempted to drive in the skirt pegs that I realized the tent we brought with us wasn't the "all-weather tent" it was advertised to be. This Swiss-made gem was not meant for winter in the northern part of Alaska. The ground that had been cleared of the upper layer snow was frozen solid and the small pegs would just chip away a little bit of crusty ground as I tried to insert them. If I exerted more effort, the pegs would only bend. The tent skirts

flapped in the wind. The temperature was somewhere between -30°F and -40°F. I was tired, and getting nowhere.

We couldn't just sleep out in the cold, totally exposed. I had to figure out something. Looking around I found some dried pine logs lying near us. Perhaps if we chopped them up so that they were equal in size they could be placed at right angles to each other in the area designated for the tent. Two logs perpendicular to each other would lie on top of two others also perpendicular to each other. They would form a square around the center tent pole. Using the pulling straps from our sleds, I could secure the tent skirts to the logs, keep the tent in place, and pack snow around the area of the logs that were lifted off the ground to close the space and provide insulation. But the straps were slippery and the holes at the edges of the tent that I had to pass the straps through were small, requiring fine motor skill. I had to take off my gloves to pass the leather straps through the holes and around the logs, and quickly lost feeling in my fingers. After fourteen hours of hiking, my body's energy reserves had dwindled to almost nothing. Tobias had to get that fire going quickly.

In the forests of Alaska there are always a lot of dry, dead, standing trees, which we always used first to build a fire. But if we couldn't find any dead wood nearby, we found that during the winter in Alaska live tree limbs were not wet at all, and we could easily break off branches if we were desperate to build a fire. Nevertheless, we always looked for dead trees first, and with the axe chopped them down and cut them up into nice-sized logs. Using the buck knife, we shaved off pieces of wood for kindling from one of the logs. Usually we needed only one match from my film roll container to create a flame.

Building the fire itself wasn't a problem. What took time and energy was clearing a large enough area of loose snow from the place where we wanted to start the fire. If the diameter of the area cleared away were any smaller than about six feet, melting snow around the fire would put out the flames. So while I set about "building" the tent on this first night, Tobias set about shoveling snow to create a valley for the fire. After that he had to make sure he had different-sized pieces of wood ready to add to the kindling. Thankfully there was no wind on the south side of the

Ray Mountains, and the fire burned steadily throughout the night.

The next essential requirement was to melt snow for drinking water. We did not take time to stop during the day and melt snow so that we could fill up our thermoses. Melting snow over a fire takes much time. You must fill up a pot with snow, and wait ten to fifteen minutes while the heat changes the snow into water. The discouraging part was that there would be little water left in the pot to show for all the snow we had put into it. On that first day, after walking for almost fourteen hours, we each had drunk only one liter of water. By the end of the day, we were quite thirsty. That night much time was spent melting snow and drinking many more liters of water to get adequately hydrated.

The fire was mostly used to warm our bodies and to melt snow for drinking water. We did not spend time cooking. Dinner consisted of the same dried fruits, nuts and berries that we nibbled on during the day. We also made pine needle tea to drink. The recipe is easy, by the way:

1. Break off a twig of pine needles from tree

2. Place twig in thermos

3. Pour hot water into thermos and steep

4. Drink

We had brought along our special air mattresses, expecting that they'd provide cushioning as well as insulation between our sleeping bags and the frigid tundra. But during cabin usage our breath had introduced moisture into them and now, outside, the air mattresses froze, rendering them useless. Tobias said he might sleep by the fire. That was craziness. A person could never stay warm enough exposed all night to -30°F temperatures, fire or no fire. He would not sleep the whole night. And Tobias really needed energy for the next day's hike, and the next. I broke off a pine branch, and then another. Pine branches snap quite easily in such cold weather. Tobias helped, and we laid the branches on the floor of our tent. We packed them tightly, creating almost a foot of insulation above the tundra floor before laying our sleeping bags on top. Besides providing wonderful insulation from the frozen tundra, the pine branches enabled sweet-smelling dreams and a

well-needed rest for both of us.

Nevertheless, sleeping in any temperature below zero requires a lot of energy. Our thermometer at night outside was reading -30°F to -35°F, and inside the tent it reached a cozy -14°F. Whatever either of us expected would happen during the night, neither of us expected to be rewarded with the magical experience we awoke to in the morning. Ice crystals refracting colors of the rainbow hung in varying lengths all around us. Our tent had become a crystal palace. Vapor from our breathing, held in by the tent's fabric, had condensed and frozen. Lying in awe, neither one of us wanted to move a muscle, recognizing that any movement would cause the magic palace to come crashing down upon us.

But move we did to begin the second day's journey, this time through deep snow and thick forest. Sometimes I would be ahead, plodding through snow that reached the knees, having to break away tree branch after tree branch that blocked our way. It was quite laborious, and would have produced a lot of dangerous sweat if dressed improperly. On my upper body I wore only a cotton t-shirt, a long sleeve cotton shirt over that, and a cotton jacket that zipped up to my neck. From the waist down I wore cotton long-underwear and wool trousers. Inside the bunny boots my feet were dressed in wool socks, which kept my feet quite warm. Of course I also wore a wool cap on my head and a wool scarf wrapped about my neck, pulled up to cover my nose. I carried a down jacket in my backpack to put on when we stopped to rest. Tobias dressed similarly. We adjusted our pace so that we wouldn't build up a sweat that would wet and then freeze our clothes. In order to keep us both from overworking, Tobias and I had to take turns being the trailblazer. Hour by hour we switched positions as we went forward. This was the first time that Tobias had ever taken the lead in anything we did together. But he had to. We had to conserve energy.

Our goal was to reach the Yukon Bridge within seven days... ten at the most. From there we knew we could find a safe, wide pathway back to Fairbanks.

On the third day we came to a crossroads of sorts. You must understand that it was Tobias' decision to walk out of the mountains

at this time almost as much as it was mine. We talked together about why we should or shouldn't do it. We came to an agreement that it would be a good idea to do a trial run for the way we would walk out in the spring. We needed to see where the rivers would flow, at what pace, and if the land would be hard snow, wet marsh, or bush-filled. So Tobias and I agreed to a walkout in November as a trial run for the spring. Fortunately there was good reason --- my tooth ache --- to test our pathway intention.

So when Tobias insisted that we descend into the valley along the right ridge of the mountain, I stood amazed. This was the first time Tobias had exercised any leadership quality. In fact, this was the first time Tobias initiated an opinion of anything. Even though my sense urged me to go left into the valley, I demurred to his instinct.

To the right the snow was deep and the trekking arduous. Again and again we fell into narrow rock indentations that were hard to avoid. Tobias predicted that we'd reach one of the Yukon finger rivers by day's end, but after thirteen hours of walking, disappointment turned into full-blown discouragement when we found ourselves still on the ridge. That night we were far from any bridge, any river and any hope of reaching Fairbanks soon. We were in deep woods, in temperatures of -30°F or below.

After putting up the tent and building the fire, Tobias was anxious to get into his sleeping bag. We had not yet melted any water or eaten any dinner.

"Tell your dentist hello for me," he said, and slipped into the tent.

I knew then that he was at a dangerous stage. I hurried to get some snow melted so he could drink, and insisted he come out by the fire to eat something.

To get to the Yukon Bridge we had to first get to the Yukon River, and when we came upon a steep and snowy bank on the fifth day, we figured that the narrow river below had to flow into the Yukon. In wilderness wisdom, rivers are like highways, the best trails to follow to lead a person toward civilization, with less obstruction than going through a forest. Tobias and I learned that during the winter, river ice in the Yukon could get as thick as six feet, and that sometimes people

drove cars over it. We figured that the small river we reached after sliding down its bank would be able to hold our weight and more.

But I was wrong. I had not opened myself up to the river's vibrations. I did not feel the change in ice thickness, and suddenly, the ice cracked and my feet and lower body fell right through the frozen surface of the river. Immediately I tried to grab onto the jagged edges of the hole through which I had fallen, but the edges were cold and slippery. I...couldn't...manage...to pull myself up... so it was with arms spread wide that I prevented myself from falling completely into the frigid waters below. Underneath I was kicking and swaying, but eerily felt no water resistance... I heard no sound of splashing... I felt no wetness seep into my feet or through my trousers. Was I was still dry? What craziness was this? Not being wet caused my breathing to return to normal, and after some minutes it dawned on us that we had come across the Big Salt River, and the saltiness of this river had caused the ice to melt from below. The water level was five or six feet lower than the river ice.

After climbing back up to safety, a feeling of thankfulness welled up inside me like I had never known before. So I gave thanks, even without knowing exactly to whom.

Later, Tobias and I were able to detect which parts of the river ice were solid and avoided dangerously thin spots. Traveling with such intense concentration made the trip much longer than anticipated and forced us to set up camp for another night along the river.

On the sixth day, there still was no indication that the Yukon River was anywhere near us. Tobias was starting to panic. But instead of retreating inward, he started to talk.

"I saw some cabins around here, from the helicopter, on the flight up, I think," he said. "Somewhere around here, I'm sure of it."

Tobias was beginning to sound like me. But without another option, I had to let him lead us.

Still, the next night, we were forced to set up camp again along the river. Once more we chopped up pine logs to form a leggo-log square so the skirt of the tent could be secured. We cleared the

snow and made a fire well, built the fire and melted the snow. We rehydrated ourselves, made pine needle tea to warm us from the inside, and had something to eat. Then came time for the part of the day I dreaded: unzipping my outer jacket before burrowing into the sleeping bag. Arctic temperatures had been hovering around -36°F, and each night as I yanked apart the zipper's metal teeth, more and more beard hairs that had frozen to the zipper got pulled from my chin with ever-increasing pain. Each time, pin-pricks of wet blood appeared, then froze. Across my cheeks and chin hairless patches covered in blood were getting bigger and bigger. Between my tooth and my face, I was ready to cut my head off.

The next morning we continued cautiously along the river, comforted in the fact that at least we had trained our eyes in summer to recognize evidence of human intervention on the riverbank. Such evidence would indicate that a cabin had been built somewhere nearby. Without whistling or singing we trudged along, maintaining a steady pace.

Rivers in Alaska are not "clean" rivers as they are in more temperate parts of the world. Clean rivers are smooth ribbons of water on which boats can easily glide when the waters are liquid because there are no obstructions. A river break-up always causes havoc in Alaskan river waters, even changing a river's shape and substance, making them very "unclean". On the Big Salt River there were tree logs and branches and frozen chunks of ice that had been caught in the onslaught of the river's rushing waters in spring, and those pieces of broken bits of forest and ice were left to be refrozen in winter.

After many hours of skirting around logs and ice chunks, we came upon signs of cleared brush and thinned out foliage on the bank at a bend in the river, so we climbed up the bank and shuffled our way inland. Finally, there was a cabin.

It was unoccupied, but filled with some clothing and lots of boxes. Boxes everywhere, some with labels addressed to a Mr. Will Lovell. One day I'd have to ask Mr. Will Lovell why his cabin was full of so many boxes, but presently I was just grateful that we had found a place where we could warm up our bodies. And dry out

our belongings. Neither one of us wanted to admit to the other that everything was wet from sweat and snow, and we had become chilled to the bone. Finding two small spaces to place our sleeping bags was the least of our worries.

The cabin was actually a nice and comfortable cabin for a trapper. We looked around and checked out the traps Will Lovell used for his work. Behind some boxes next to the sink was a radio, but the battery was missing. With such a promising sign as a radio, we figured surely there must be a battery somewhere.

In Alaska there was a communication system called "Pipeline to the North". It was used by all the people out in the bush to place orders for food, clothing, or emergency help. We needed to use it for the last thing. Emergency help. Our food was almost gone and the excruciating pain in my tooth had spread to the rest of my jaw.

We looked around outside and found a shed located about a hundred feet from the main cabin. Inside the shed was a generator and a supply of batteries. Now I had something to work with! I made sure there was enough water in the generator, hooked up a battery to the generator, and after several hours of charging, inserted the regenerated battery into the radio. With great excitement I turned the radio dial to ON.

Suddenly, from the back of the rusty contraption a spark and a cloud of gray smoke burst forth. Then: nothing. Our charged battery had killed the radio.

I was flabbergasted.

Tobias lifted his shoulders and turned away.

I pulled the radio towards me and pried open the back of the battery compartment. Looking inside I found a coiled wire that had separated from its metal plate. This I attached once again to its mooring, closed the compartment and tried the radio once more. It turned on!

I took the microphone. "Hello. Hello," I said.

"Ralph here," another voice answered. A voice! A voice! A person!

I told the operator where we were.

"I know the place," Ralph answered.

"Can you organize a plane to pick us up?" I asked him.

'What's with that 'organize' and all? You guys European?" he asked.

I told him we were from Switzerland.

"I knew it," he said. "All righty. I can have someone out there to pick you up two days from now. In the morning. At nine in the morning."

Tobias and I looked at each other and laughed out loud. Even though I had been using my watch to measure out our days, there was no time in the wilderness. No one uses a clock out in the middle of nowhere. We had never seen anyone operate on a time schedule anywhere in Alaska.

"You got that?" the voice on the radio cracked.

"Got it," I answered, and the radio quieted.

Tobias and I immediately went outside and started building a landing strip.

We both realized that it could take another six days to get back to Fairbanks if we continued walking. I was grateful in my heart that Tobias had remembered where he had seen the cabins during the helicopter flight from Fairbanks.

On the morning of the second day after the radio contact, I was in the outhouse when I heard a buzzing sound. It got louder and louder, and I realized the sound was the engine of our rescue jet. I looked at my watch. The time showed five minutes before nine.

The plane landed expertly on our runway. After it had come to a stop, out jumped a grizzled, gray-haired man. He had to be over seventy years old. Everything's unexpected in Alaska. He smiled. "Name's Harold," he said as he walked toward us.

We put our bags inside the aircraft. Harold jumped into his seat and threw us out some ropes.

"You're gonna have to help me turn this here piece of equipment around," he announced with a glint in his eye. "Run along the plane with me, and when I get down to the end of that piece of short runway y'all stamped out, pull the tail around to the right."

We did as he said, and he, with our muscle, expertly turned the plane 180 degrees. We hopped inside, and off we went.

The flight back to Fairbanks was about an hour and a half long. We surprised Peter and Fabienne with our appearance, saw their twitching noses, and headed right for the showers at the University. I also shaved. Forty-three times I had resolved to cut my whole darn beard off when I got back to civilization, and now here I was.

Tobias and I brought along all of our dirty clothes to wash after the shower, since the laundromat was close to the university. Each of us filled a machine and sat back to watch the hypnotic rotation of our clothes going round and round in the washer drums, happy to be alive, happy to be safe, happy to be warm. I looked out the window. "Hmm," I said under my breath. Tobias looked out the window. "Hmm," he said under his breath. Immediately we both got out of our seats, went through the door and headed for the Foodland Grocery story across the parking lot. After a couple of months in the wilderness, and even though living through minus thirty degree weather, the first thing we craved upon being back in the city was Häagen-Dazs ice cream. That was a dream to break the monotony of the washer machine.

After doing the laundry we decided to look for Will Lovell to thank him for the use of his cabin along the Big Salt River. We went to both his home and work addresses, but couldn't find him at either place. So we left him some money and a note, expressing gratefulness for his hospitality. On the note we said he should put to good use the Stanley thermos I had left on his table. It was comfortable to carry and sturdy, too. I would miss it.

The next day I saw the dentist that Peter recommended.

"How shall I fix your tooth?" she asked. "Shall I do it the way we do here in Alaska, or the way it has been done before?"

"What's the difference?" I asked.

"The method with which you had your cavity fixed in Switzerland hasn't been used here in twenty years," she answered.

At that moment I decided to change dentists when I returned to Zurich.

| 27 |

HEADING BACK

During the flight from the Big Salt River to Fairbanks, Tobias and I made a decision. We knew we would not be able to walk back into the mountains when my tooth was fixed, and taking a helicopter would be too expensive. Harold had already given us a price of $200 for the flight from Big Salt River to Fairbanks. Perhaps he would chauffeur us into the Ray Mountains again in a few days for the same price.

"I wouldn't want to do that," he said, staring out at the horizon.

I explained that there was an open area near our cabin where a helicopter we hired had landed. I told him I noticed that there was quite a bit of hard-packed snow on the ground when we left. "You could use that for a runway," I offered. "I'm sure that area could be used as a runway."

"I wouldn't want to do that," he said again, then turned to me with a glimpse of humor in his eyes and added, "but I will." Harold agreed to charge us $200 for the flight back in.

You never know what to expect in Alaska.

A week later we joined Harold at the airport. We packed our stuff into the aircraft, and took off with Harold at the controls and no map in sight. He headed northeast, and after staying the course for two hours, made a slight left turn to the west. When Harold dropped lower over the mountains, we saw it. Our little valley. Lots of snow drifts had accumulated, and my heart stopped.

He's not going to be able to land, I thought.

Harold approached the snowy area I indicated as the landing strip and allowed the plane to turn in a wide circle. We descended in a spiral, coming closer and closer to the ground. As soon as the plane touched the snow, Harold reversed the engine's thrust and quickly, miraculously, was able to stop the plane.

We invited him for coffee. He took a long look at the sky. "No. I'd better be leavin'," he said. We helped him turn the plane with the ropes, well acquainted with how it all worked this time, and he took off. He said good-bye by shaking his wings and then he was gone. One hour after he left, the next storm hit our cabin. It was a storm that lasted several days, which gave us plenty of time to reorder the cabin and establish a routine.

1. My plan for what to do in the wilderness was quite simple:

2. Do whatever was needed to be done to eat and stay warm.

3. Explore the valley and the mountains.

4. Observe the animals in their habitats.

5. Figure out more about myself.

At the beginning Tobias appeared to have no desire to go anywhere near number four with me. He never mentioned one thing he was learning or had figured out about himself. At least not until we started doing wood sculptures together.

I had been collecting small, interesting blocks of pinewood for a few weeks, stacking them in one corner of the cabin. When we returned to the cabin in December, there were frequent storms, which gave us plenty of time to do some creative woodworking.

Initially, Tobias sat nearby as I worked and silently watched. Eventually he pulled out his own Swiss knife, chose his own piece of wood, and began chipping away. I mentioned that he might want to turn the knife away from him and make sure he was shaving along the grain. He listened and watched and copied well.

As the hours passed, relaxation set in and words began to trickle out.

"I've been thinking about what kind of profession I should choose for myself," he said. "You know, when I get back to Switzerland."

Before leaving St. Gallen Tobias had been trained as a post office worker. It was a nice, safe job, perhaps something his mother had chosen for him.

"I was thinking about becoming a baker," Tobias volunteered as a surprising bit of personal information. Since returning to the mountains we had been daring each other to come up with different kinds of muffins or cookies each time we made a batch. Tobias' last batch of muffins, made with wheat, oats, dried blueberries, cranberries, chopped walnuts, and pumpkin seeds had been quite creative. "I have an uncle who is a baker. He makes sweets."

There were times that I had wanted to shake Tobias hard to get any sound to come out of him, and now he was volunteering information. I wondered how I could keep the flow coming.

"A baker, huh?" I repeated.

"Um-hum."

"Doing the job of a baker would be challenging for me," I went on.

"How do you mean?"

"Well, as I see it, a person would have to wake up at two or three in the morning --- pretty much every morning --- because people do like their bread and tarts to be fresh."

Tobias smiled.

"And what about friends?" I asked.

Tobias looked at me as if I didn't know what in the world I was talking about. "What do friends have to do with it?" he asked back.

"Well, a baker is on opposite sides of the daily schedule that all his friends have. While they'd be out having a nice dinner and a drink at the bar, he'd be home in bed waiting for a wake-up alarm to go off. His friends would be going to bed just as he'd be getting up."

"Ah. Didn't think of that," Tobias admitted. He bent his bearded face and chipped away a few more pieces from his woodblock. "My uncle doesn't seem to mind it too much. Getting up early, I mean."

"But I wonder when he gets a chance to spend any time with anybody?" I said more as a statement than a question. I continued sanding my wood.

Tobias smoothed one end of the bear he was carving with his thumb. "I guess my uncle doesn't have many friends. I guess you're right there."

"Have you worked with him at his shop at all?" I asked.

"Yeah. Once or twice during my vacation. I think he's a really nice guy."

I figured it was something like that. That Tobias really liked the uncle more than the profession.

I learned as I worked with Tobias that he was quite intelligent. He had a quick mind. Once shown how to do something, he remembered well. But when Tobias ground our grain, his mind seemed always somewhere else. I figured that being a baker would easily bore him.

He brought up being a house builder. Then it was my turn to smile. Immediately I thought of the time here in the mountains when he nearly cut his thumb off with the axe. Tobias hadn't wanted to show me the wound. I was out when the accident happened, and when I returned he tried to hide his thumb behind his back.

I realized as we talked and worked that his parents had kept him from many basic experiences that would have let him know for himself what things he could be good at, what things he could dedicate his life to. As a child he could have found out much more about himself.

His parents cheated him by preventing him from doing this.

INTO THE STREAM

nly two snowstorms tumbled into our valley in November, but windstorms came frequently, constantly rearranging the scenery. After each noisy whirlwind died down, Tobias and I would crunch our way into the outdoor "garden" to observe any new piece of artwork on display. What unusual snow sculptures had been formed? What challenging snowdrifts were there to climb?

But windstorm or no, after returning to the cabin from Fairbanks, it was only after restoring order to our living space and establishing a routine that we allowed ourselves to embark on a nice, long hike. By now we were well aware that in temperatures like -30°F, having wet boots or wet trousers could cost a person a foot or a leg, so we always took care to stay dry.

We initiated the hike along the creek near our cabin and soon became mesmerized by the peaceful beauty of the valley below, where the creek had grown into a frozen river that opened wide and spread out over quite a distance.

Wind had blown away snow from several chunks of stacked river ice, most of which was artfully arranged into colorful ice structures that refracted varying intensities of blues and greens. The structures and their colors hypnotized us, enjoining us to stay and examine the varying hues more carefully.

Over a narrower part of the river we spotted what looked like

a beaver dam and were curious to see if beavers still lived inside. Beavers' teeth create interesting patterns when they gnaw down trees, and I always enjoyed studying the marks their teeth leave on the trunks of trees they fell. Beavers are clever architects, too, building structures which maintain their positions despite the fact that water constantly tries to disturb their construction. We stepped across the frozen river to the beaver castle to examine it more closely.

All of a sudden the ice on which we were stepping broke right through and one of my legs fell into the stream below.

A second time Tobias remained safe while a part of me --- this time --- definitely did not.

And this time I felt the wetness. It didn't feel as cold as I expected, so, foolishly or not, I kept my leg in the water while thinking what I should do.

Should I ask Tobias to go build a fire?

Would I be safe if Tobias went to gather wood while I stayed low with my leg in the water?

Did I have to look out for more ice breaking off, in which case my whole body might fall into the water?

Should we both hurry back to the cabin?

Should Tobias go back to the cabin alone to get a fire ready there?

It was all unclear. I finally let out a "Shit!" but not in English.

I was afraid yet again. I recognized the emotion now. The first requirement for surviving in the wilderness in the wintertime is to stay dry. Being submerged in water, or just becoming wet from sweating too much, is one of the most dangerous things that can happen.

In Switzerland I'd trampled across dozens of frozen lakes and streams. I had become quite good at knowing where it was safe to walk and where it wasn't. Now, in Alaska, something that I thought could never happen, happened. I believed I'd be able to sense any spot of ice that couldn't carry me. I knew ice was dangerous, even before falling through it on the Salt River during the walkout. I

knew it was dangerous even before Harold-the-Pilot offered me his assessment regarding ice. "If I can, I avoid landing on it," he said. "Never sure if it will hold," he said. "Difficult thing to figure out," he said. Terse words. They came back at me like bullets.

Tobias was as shocked as I was. "Should I build a fire?" he asked.

If I kept my leg in the water while Tobias built a fire, it could freeze.

If I pulled my leg out of the water and began to walk back to the cabin in -35°F weather, my leg and foot would surely freeze in the open air. I might not even be able to reach the cabin --- might not even be able to drag a frozen leg there. And then I'd have to wait for Tobias to get the fire going in the cabin. If Tobias ran on ahead to get the fire ready so that it would be waiting for me when I got there, I would be all alone on the hike back and most surely would not be able to make it without his help.

"Should I build a fire?" Tobias repeated.

Let me think.

"Shall I run back to the cabin to start the fire?" he persisted. He saw I was nervous. He saw I was worried. He saw my eyes --- and felt my nervousness. My fear penetrated him. I could lose my foot.

Let me think.

I needed divine intervention, but the thought occurred to me that if I wasted time praying, my foot would freeze solid.

I didn't pray.

In stress situations, many people fail to come up with any ideas. The mind goes blank. The body freezes. What happens normally is exactly what happened when I met my first grizzly bear.

But here, now, in the seconds after I realized I needed divine intervention, two thoughts crystallized. The first thought was that I was wearing bunny boots. The second thought was that there was the possibility that I could dry my trousers with snow. Snow in the arctic region of Alaska in winter is very dry. It will absorb moisture.

So in the most stressed of moments I was able to come up with a solution. And then I was able to act on it.

Immediately I climbed out of the hole in the stream and quickly began rubbing dry snow on very wet trousers. Then I sat down to hold my foot up so that the water would drain out of my boot.

What if I wrap my down coat around my trousers, to prevent my leg from freezing? I could walk back to the cabin like that. I believed the cold on my upper body would be tolerable because that part of me was dry. I wrapped the coat around my leg and Tobias and I headed home.

I walked in boots with wet socks and left-over water inside, but nothing froze. My leg did not freeze up either.

It didn't take me long to realize that there was no real pending danger.

Experience always helps when seeking a solution. But even with experience you can do the wrong thing.

Out of that broken stream I felt a strong pull by something --- or someone --- other than myself.

I couldn't call it luck this time. This time it was more than luck that saved me. I knew luck wouldn't have gotten me safely back to the cabin. So I gave thanks to that someone I felt was watching over me... to that someone who managed to keep me safe when the situation called for the impossible.

CHRISTMAS

As the sun's slivers of light weakened and its fading orb sank slowly below the horizon, not to shine brightly again until springtime, the moon's glow grew and brightened across a blue to violet to black sky. On cloudless or windless days we were always saved from total darkness. A moon over snow-covered landscape allows for very usable light.

But three days before Christmas there was no moon shining as increasingly robust winds rolled over the south side of the mountains into the valley. The storm forced us to tightly secure the window shutters and remain inside the cabin. At night complete darkness inside coupled with the growing storm outside made me feel as if I were a passenger on a high speed train racing through a tunnel, where there were engine sounds all around and no way to tell the beginning from the end.

By day we read and whittled wood, all the while relighting candles after they shook and blew out, until finally the storm spent itself out on Christmas Eve. Christmas morning announced itself with a complete and lovely silence. Then the murmur of the stream that passed by our cabin drifted gently through the windows, and its peaceful whispers caused me to heave great sighs of relief.

I slipped out of my sleeping bag, donned the pilot trousers, boots and down jacket and crept outside. The air was bracingly cold, but the sky was clear and sparkling with stars, as if an army of Swiss jewelers had just shined and hung their diamonds there.

Tobias and I hadn't planned to give each other presents, but we did decorate the table and countertop with pine wreaths and candles to celebrate the holiday. From the coldest corner of the cabin wine was brought forth. It was the same bottle we had left uncorked before our walkout and had kept frozen until this day, because this was the day for which it was originally intended. Tobias moved the bottle closer to the fire for gentle defrosting. We made apple pie from dried apples that became sweet when water was added. And we sang two songs, or as much as we could remember of each one.

What would have made the celebration extra special would have been the appearance of the Aurora Borealis, Alaska's famous Northern Lights, displayed so frequently in the fall --- in October and November --- but forlornly absent in late December. The Ray Mountains' Northern Lights were swaths of sparkling colors --- deep to light blues, vibrant to soft greens, even pink to crimson to violet --- that dashed and swirled upon a velvet curtain all around us, as if they were glorious angels. Being touched by them always left me feeling like a child. I would stand motionless, with big eyes and an open mouth.

The Eskimos say that the Northern Lights are actually the spirits of their dead. "If you listen, you can hear their whispering," they say.

I did always have the feeling that while the Lights performed their ballet, something else was present, but I never heard any whispering. What was present was not something that you could record with an audio or video camera, but you could definitely sense it.

On the night before our helicopter flight to the mountains, after dropping off Tobias at the Yukon Bridge, Northern Lights accompanied me all the way back to Fairbanks. I stopped during part of their show and just sat and watched. I studied physics in school and can explain what the phenomenon is, but there was something else happening. Physics cannot explain the effect the Northern Lights can exert on a person. The Lights touched me. They permeated my being.

Tobias and I talked about how beautiful the scene always was. I stood beside him once and watched him look at the Lights. His face became transformed. He was totally thrilled, totally alive, totally aware. Just not of me.

| 30 |

JANUARY STORMS

Our days in the mountains were either blessed with blissful silence, or cursed with the booming racket of a storm. More days and nights were filled with storms than without. After sunlight had decreased to nothing by the end of November, wind steadily increased through December and January. Darkness didn't make the Alaskan cold feel colder, but the wind surely did. If we found ourselves outside in a storm for even an hour, we would have frozen. Sometimes just being out for thirty minutes could immobilize us. It was very dangerous.

It was also extremely frustrating and confusing, since storm warnings were infrequent.

When the first storm hit, our cabin shook as if it were going to be unplugged from the ground. The wind almost broke through the plastic sheeting tacked over the windows, even though we had secured heavy wooden shutters over the plastic. Luckily the plastic survived the battle, because we had no extra. Our supplies did include one roll of footy tape, which could have been used over the windows if needed. We originally bought it to use for emergency leaks in the canoe. The tape was black and would have given a dark and closed-in feeling to the cabin, so thankfully it was never required.

Even so my mind would darken as I felt the fury of the storms and deliberated over what could cause such rage. My thoughts kept

going back to that Ruler of the Air the Eskimo talked about at the Fairbanks coffee shop. Was I really in the middle of a spiritual battle? I comprehended more fully why the Indians had warned Tobias and me about the "ghosts" who lived in the Ray Mountains. The atmosphere was dangerously electric, and unsettling to the core.

Being surrounded by the howling winds and furious rattling of tiny snow pellets against the walls of the cabin provided plenty of time to comprehend why the Indians wouldn't want to live here. But I couldn't understand why Robert Agen did. Eventually I figured that Robert Agen must have bought his piece of property during the summertime. He must have never seen the winter before building the cabins. He probably planned on renting out the cabins regularly, thinking the area would be a fine place for wilderness hikers. Perhaps he hadn't gotten the chance to meet any Indians who might have directed him away from the Ray Mountains. I thought this might have been the case until I admitted that I, myself, had been lucky enough to meet some Indians, and yet here I was in the melancholic mountains anyway. Well, everyone has to learn for himself. I had already determined that I would never come back. Maybe Robert Agen had concluded the same thing.

Beginning with the third week of January I turned irascible because of a storm that was lasting way too long. Again and again the wind would rise up one side of one of the mountains and fall down the other. Almost two weeks passed and still the storm raged. Cabin fever overcame me, emotionally and physically. I yanked on my pilot trousers and threw on my jacket and cap and stomped out to face my nemesis.

"You stupid, bloody storm!" I screamed into the wind. "You stupid, stupid, stupid, bloody storm!" I pounded my feet and screamed some more. That was the extent of my cursing vocabulary in English. And oddly, weirdly, the next day, the storm dissipated.

More words than normal trickled out of Tobias in the wintertime. But during many of the storms, he still refused to talk about more than what he might ultimately dedicate himself to for a living. Sometimes I wanted to shake other thoughts out of him,

because in winter in the wilderness in the middle of a storm, you need something else to hold onto besides yourself.

At the end, the winter experience turned out a little differently than expected. It was more intense because of the storms.

The intensity had to do with self-exploration. I had to listen to myself, and couldn't keep from imagining what was going on inside of Tobias.

I was forced to ask questions I had avoided up until that point. Where had my father gone? Was there a purpose to why he had been taken before I was ready to let him go? Where had I come from? Where would I end up? Why did I still have full use of a right leg that should have been frozen to death in the stream? What was I here on earth for?

When the storms stopped, the intensity lessened, and there were always beautiful moments of silence.

One of the most enchanting occurred while I stood with arms held wide on top of one of those mountains surrounding our valley, looking out as far as I could. Wherever I gazed the whole sky and earth were completely void of any other human soul. No sound could be heard, and I was at peace.

| 31 |

ALONE IN WINTER

2001, *A Space Odyssey* was a book that challenged my thinking about what it would be like to fly off into outer space, and it was my companion as I first flew off to wander into Alaska. But there were other books that I discovered in Robert Agen's tiny mountain library that challenged me to think much more profoundly about life on this planet, in my own earthly space.

John Steinbeck drew me into his book *East of Eden* just like our measured supply of popcorn kernels drew to itself a tiny, short-tailed red lemming that was burrowed under our cabin. No matter how Tobias or I tried to intimidate the lemming with a booming voice or a hand that swatted him away, the lemming came searching for popcorn kernels every day without fail. Steinbeck's description of the warm hills in the California valley where his unusual characters lived made me want to visit it every day without fail, too. I was reading the book during a period of storms, a period in which I spent many hours indoors contemplating my existence. It was a tense time for me as I explored what kind of person I was and the kind I wanted to be. What were the things I valued? What qualities were unimportant?

East of Eden featured Cathy Ames, one of the main characters, as more than just a person who happened to do a few bad things. She was a person who lied to, stole from, cheated, tortured or killed whomever got in the way of her plans, and furthermore seemed to feel no remorse for any of those things. I became fascinated with

her.

From watching small children on the playground who shove others out of the way when they want the swing, or who lie to the teacher when she asks about undone homework or cheating on a test, I had already come to understand that human beings who live upon this earth have their shortcomings. But this Cathy displayed more than shortcomings. She appeared to be tarnished through and through, and in a way, I admired her. I figured that it required quite a bit of courage for Cathy to live out her desires for personal freedom and revenge. Surely there'd be awful consequences for living such a life and a person would have to be strong to face such consequences.

Usually a human in any modern, civilized society today will make an effort to subdue evil tendencies, hide them, or ignore them. Usually a person likes to be liked and doesn't display an evil persona to family and friends, or go all out and put negative characteristics on parade for all the world to see. But Cathy did. She was Cathy through and through, and never lied to herself about who she was. What a very brave person she was, indeed.

What would it be like to live as she lived, doing whatever she pleased?

What kind of person does whatever he or she pleases?

I had never known anyone in my life who did whatever he or she wanted to do, good or bad, and not consider the effect such actions or decisions would have on others. I especially never thought it was possible to harm another person and not have to suffer the consequences for it.

So I began to ask myself, *Why shouldn't I just do whatever I wanted?* I was always bending over backwards to do what others expected of me, what others wanted me to do. Why was I always trying to please everyone else instead of just trying to please myself? Trying to please others all the time was a lot of work. Why should I continue?

Reading further into *East of Eden*, I learned that this woman, this Cathy, this character in the book who later called herself Kate, was forced to face the earthly consequences of her evil

choices. Cathy/Kate grew weak and sallow and ugly as her body painfully deteriorated. She had neither family, nor friends, nor loyal employees to comfort or help her. She was hated and despised by all.

Okay. Well.

Learning about the results that befell her made me recognize that there just might be dire consequences for any illicit behavior on my part, too. Cathy's/Kate's behavior led to outcomes that, when described so vividly, frightened me. I surely didn't want to spend half of my life as she spent hers. Furthermore, I pondered, if I purposefully committed evil acts throughout my lifetime, what would happen to me in the end, when my life was over? Was the Bible true when it said that leading such a life separated a person from God for eternity? I eventually resolved not to be the kind of person to reach heaven's gates, if in fact they really existed, carrying obnoxious and foul baggage with me. (But what I didn't understand at the time was this: I didn't have the power to make sure my baggage was cleaned out simply because I resolved it.)

Another of the main characters in *East of Eden* that I admired was Adam, the man Cathy married. Some might consider Adam weak because he let others manipulate him, and I might agree, but I didn't consider him a coward. Adam was only weak because he was born with a more passive personality that didn't allow him to harm anyone. When attacked he was unable to fight back. But not fighting back takes a kind of courage, too. Adam didn't try to pretend that he was someone other than who he was. He didn't lie, he didn't make up stories about what kind of person he was, nor did he make up stories about his past, re-inventing himself, as his father did. Adam's father was the real coward, I thought, because his father did lie about the kind of man he was. He pretended to be someone he was not. I could never admire such a person.

Tobias' mother was a coward. To the world she pretended to be a confident, generous and loving parent, because every day she cooked her son's food, sewed his clothing, and let him live in her house. But this was only a façade that prevented anyone from seeing what she was really like: insecure, selfish and afraid. Mrs. Senn was not only afraid to let her son travel to Alaska, she was

afraid to let him out of her sight. She was afraid to let her son wander off into the world because she couldn't control him from afar, and controlling him made her feel powerful and important. Controlling Tobias gave her a purpose. Mrs. Senn would deny her son his freedom so that she could continue experiencing her power. But of course she never would have admitted that she was controlling. If she had, I would have called her courageous, because at least she would have recognized what lay beneath the surface. Instead, as she kept the house and cooked the meals and talked to her husband, all the while smiling her wooden smile, she never admitted, even to herself, that she was selfish, that she was unkind, or that she was destroying Tobias' life which had been entrusted to her. I would call this a type of hate, and Mrs. Senn would have never admitted that she had hate in her heart.

She had hate in her heart for me, too, because I was taking her son away. I could see it, but she would have denied it. Perhaps if I had given in to her request and encouraged Tobias to stay in Switzerland, she would have smiled her wooden smile and pretended love, but it would have only been pretense because she hated me for even bringing the idea of escape to Tobias. A coward is one who pretends rather than one who shows his or her true personality. A coward would rather lie than reveal the sickness that resides in the heart.

Before Alaska, I was a coward who pretended to be something other than who I really was.

I was a coward because even though I had been afraid of many things, I displayed a persona of fearlessness. As often as possible, I removed myself from situations in which I would have had to admit fear. There was always a place where I could go to reaffirm to myself that I was sound and strong and in control. That place existed anywhere in the mountains. It was when I was in the city, at home or at work, surrounded by people, that I felt insecure and afraid.

Relating to people was what exposed me. The successes of others in my chosen profession made me feel insecure because from youth it had been written on my slate that I was an imposter, with nothing original to offer. The self-assurance and easy camaraderie

I noted between young men and young women as they shared activities or dated left me feeling weak and vulnerable. Ever since Reguli there had been no easy camaraderie with young women. Any scripts written inside me that could have reassured me that I had gifts to offer...in art or in life...had been erased.

I didn't show up on the doorstep of the art school in St. Gallen because my mother signed the papers for enrollment. I showed up because I thought I wouldn't pass the test. I didn't choose to become a Graphic Designer. Not at all. The truth was that at MBD I really wasn't a very good designer.

I simply followed the patterns of other artists who had come before me. I copied, changed a thing here or there, went off the grid a little, and others called it "creative". But I was incapable of generating the broad swath of the "first idea" or starting with something truly original. I could never have formulated an overall idea to create a structure such as Le Corbusier's church in Ronchamp. I excused myself by saying that there were always deadlines nipping at my heels, and these deadlines never afforded the time needed to adequately explore a solution that a truly original design required. I was very good with excuses. Were others saying I was good because I made a living at it? That isn't a satisfying enough answer for me. I should be better, I would think. But my insecurity and (what I now recognize as) fear of failure kept me from being honest and true. I wouldn't admit that I couldn't do such a project, just that I hadn't done such a project. From youth my insecurity bound me as a prisoner.

Nevertheless, I recognized that some insecurity went into remission in Basel, where teachers let me know that my thoughts had worth. The release from my personal prison continued further at MBD because of the back-and-forth conversations with Müller-Brockmann. At twenty-six years old, I was finally able to speak regularly with someone whom I trusted. Bit by bit I learned to open up, to explain myself, and to hear again, after Basel, that my instincts and thoughts had value. Still, I wasn't completely free.

Vati stunted my emotional growth by planting in me thoughts of my own unworthiness, stupidity, and failure. These thought-seeds grew into a shell that hardened itself around my soul and

prevented any positive feelings about myself to enter in.

I felt unworthy of Vati's love not because of what I did, but because of what he failed to do: he refused to hug me, and in his voice I don't ever remember hearing the sound of gentleness and acceptance. He would be gone for days on end into the mountains by himself, and when he returned, after quietly taking out his tools, he would begin a new carving in silence. I would watch and wait for his attention, his voice, or his hug, but none ever came. Vati made me feel as if I were stupid by not listening when I spoke, even though I never bothered him when he was concentrating on his calligraphy or when he was listening to a glacier. I always excused him, though, by asking myself, Why should he listen if I have nothing important to say? Vati made me feel incapable of succeeding by refusing to recognize my progress as a skier or my attempts at being a whittler. The harder I tried the more his critical looks increased. He would point out what was wrong, not what was right. You might think this is an appropriate way to learn, but when you never hear that something is pleasing, you come to believe that you can never please, that you can never be good enough, or that you will never reach the mark.

Somehow, though, after persevering again and again without my father, I became a good skier and deep inside was able to congratulate myself for making progress. So I became confident and at peace when I was in the mountains, but what happened when there was no snow? I had not learned how to navigate the rest of life. People had remained unknown glaciers and I thought I was happy to keep them that way.

After my father's years of rejection of me, I had been unable to successfully cope with anyone else's anger, criticism, or rejection of me. Any love I had offered had not been returned, so why try to offer it again? Feelings of rejection and failure caused my stomach to churn, which in turn left me feeling out of control. I didn't know how to fight off those feelings so I tried to eliminate from my life any situations that would cause them. But escapes into the wilderness not only negatively affected my artwork, they affected the rest of my life, too.

For instance, I wouldn't have said that I refused to love another person because of fear, but that's what it was. I was afraid to love. I was afraid to expose myself and to give of myself. What if this person that I left myself open to rejected me? I had loved Vati with all my heart, after all, and he had rejected me, over and over again. If I committed to being patient and kind to another person, wouldn't that person just take advantage of me? I was afraid that if I committed to denying my own desires and to putting the other person first, then I'd have to keep giving up parts of myself so that eventually there'd be nothing left of me. Like Mrs. Senn, I didn't really understand what love was about, so I maintained my own wooden façade that I lived behind. To others I appeared to be an independent guy who didn't have a care in the world and who didn't need anybody else to survive, and eventually I convinced myself to believe the lie.

If I felt any attraction for a member of the opposite sex, my fear of being rejected stopped me from pursuing that attraction. I would hide behind my tough-guy façade, and do nothing. Ultimately I wouldn't even admit to myself that feelings for a girl even existed. I didn't want to deal with loving someone. And I refused to think that I needed to be loved by anyone.

Of course I did fall in love, but if you're wondering if the object of my affection ever knew how I felt, the answer is "No."

I never told her.

She didn't approach me, either, so I felt justified in assuming she had no feelings for me.

I didn't know that voicing love for someone can turn that person's heart toward you.

I never thought that I could go after someone I liked and make my feelings known.

And in fact I never wanted to because I was convinced that I'd always find out later that there were things about that person that were...annoying...unlikeable...distasteful...or all-in-all unlovable.

I didn't know that I could choose to love that person, and didn't understand that sometimes you have to choose. Love as a feeling doesn't always come to you. Sometimes you have to go

after it. I know now that love is a verb.

There is one more thing that I can tell you I was afraid of --- something that my pride makes it hard to admit, but here it is.

Opportunities to come in contact with people who dressed and spoke differently than I did were seldom, and so I became afraid to engage strangers in a conversation. At school and in the army teachers or sergeants hovered over me, telling me what to do. They controlled the hours and days, leaving time for only small talk with the few acquaintances who happened to be near a desk or an army cot. The truth is that we Swiss keep to ourselves naturally. Other Europeans make jokes about how no one should count on a Swiss to carry on a conversation. But my shyness allowed me to puff myself up. I wore jeans and, not recognizing that jeans are a costume unto themselves, decided that everyone who dressed according to the fashion of the day was hiding something. The truth was that I was hiding my own insecurity of not knowing how to navigate in social circles where people wore suits and ties. So instead of stepping into the pond and figuring out how to communicate with differently-costumed fellow human beings, I judged them. And my feigned superiority kept me in a prison, preventing me from knowing other humans beings, artfully dressed or not, and their struggles.

At home there had been no training in the art of conversation, because with a father like mine, words in my youth were exchanged sparingly. Vati and I passed a great amount of time in the mountains where there was little need for a lot of talk. In the end I realized that it was because of my discomfort (fear) of people that I loved the mountains, where I could be alone and self-sufficient. I lived a lot inside my own head, believing without question whatever idea an authority figure had planted in there.

Before coming to Alaska I walked a very narrow path. There existed either right or wrong, black or white, and nothing in-between. Mine was a closed system. By eighteen years old, I had made all the important decisions I thought a person needed to make. In my mind there was no need to learn anything new about the way the world worked, there was no need to try to understand people better, there was no need to pursue Truth or find out if

there was any information out there about God himself that I didn't already have. With my small pack of ideas, I was my own god, the judge of what was right and wrong.

I repeatedly rationalized why others were always in the wrong. Because if they were right, I would have to admit that I might be wrong! I would have to admit that I didn't know everything! If there were other choices, if other people with different ideas than what had already been shared with me could be right, then I would have to face all kinds of emotions ...including fear...and love.

Being with other people and seeing their joy would make me have to admit that I wasn't joyful, and seeing their sadness would make me have to join in with their grief. In looking at other people's creativity or well-developed artistic skills, I'd have to admit my own imperfections.

For me to function at work or with friends I had to be perceived as perfect, infallible, and sure of every decision, and because I pretended so well I came to believe that I was infallible, perfect and all-knowing.

Of course it was all a ruse. Everyone makes mistakes, and no one knows everything. But I avoided any situation that could have possibly ended in exposing my flaws, inabilities, limitations, or fears. I also criticized people who made mistakes --- who weren't as strong as I thought I was --- and I could get really harsh with them. The smaller others could be made to look, the bigger I appeared.

My insecurity was the motor behind all the dangerous things I had done, by the way, and perhaps was doing right at that moment, sitting in an abandoned mountain cabin far away from the safety of Switzerland. I came to Alaska to prove that I really was Mr. Tough Guy, but then quickly came to see that I was just a guy. Alaska was the most perilous place on earth I had ever encountered. This dark and cold retreat in the mountains was exposing all of my vulnerabilities. During the winter in the mountains the bindings that had held my soul prisoner were beginning to loosen even more.

Before Alaska, I felt impervious to harm. I could take care of myself, and if I got into trouble there'd always be someone to

rescue me from danger. Nurses and doctors were a drive or a phone call away.

In the Alaskan mountains there was only Tobias. Sure, I could depend on Tobias to a certain degree, but he was depending on me. Out in the wilderness, a very small mishap could turn quickly into something quite hazardous, or even deadly.

The recognition of the things I needed to admit about myself didn't happen all of a sudden while reading novels huddled next to a glowing candle during winter storms in the Ray Mountains. Rather, I realized that since coming to Alaska, I was slowing down to pay attention to how I felt about the circumstances I found myself in, and the animals and people who crossed my path. It was as if my conscience awoke, and I began paying attention to it.

In the Fall, Tobias and I watched with awesome curiosity several animals as they ate and moved about. From a distance we admired a bull, a beautiful and proud male moose with a mighty rack above his head. He was graceful and strong. It was bow-hunting season and a few days later we found his remains --- his hooves, part of his skull and enough of him to know that it was our bull --- and witnessing that scene shocked and sickened my soul.

In Switzerland and up until the beginning of our time in Alaska, I had entertained the thought that if it were necessary, I would use a gun to kill a moose. But that day, upon seeing the remains of the slaughter, I decided to never shoot such a beautiful animal. I would be a respecter of life.

Nevertheless, deep inside I held onto the notion that survival in the Arctic might require killing a snow rabbit or one of those Ptarmigan white birds who sink down in the snow thinking they're invisible to predators. I rationalized that killing them would be acceptable because the process wouldn't involve a gun, just a metal tarp line set out over the ground. Any number of animals would get stuck in the tarp line, and without a single bullet being fired, would freeze to death. The only duty would be to gather up dinner each night.

But Tobias and I never set up a tarp line. Instead, when our bodies craved concentrated protein, we decided to catch, fry, and eat fish. (What would you do if you were a respecter of life but also

hungry, cold, and in need of energy?) Yet even killing a fish was hard. Luring a scale-y, living creature out of the water, watching its shimmering body squirm, and then whacking it across the head was very difficult indeed.

So we respecters of life often went one step further and contented ourselves with a simple diet of grains. Rice and whole wheat were very satisfying, and grinding wheat gives a lot of warmth to the body! For more rounded nourishment there were various dried fruits and vegetables to choose from our supplies. We had counted on sprouting alfalfa seeds for our vitamin C requirement, but sadly the alfalfa seeds froze in the jar on the first night in the mountains. So instead of the sprouted seeds, we enjoyed different kinds of jams from the berries we had picked in the fall, ate dried rose hips, and drank pine needle tea to keep any virus at bay.

It was because I intentionally watched and listened, not only with my body but also with my spirit, that I was able to learn what qualities in life I valued and which were important to maintain a healthy soul. I doubt Cathy ever allowed herself to do that.

And the lemming that lived under our cabin? He carted away so many captured kernels between his tiny sharp teeth that we finally had to do something about him. So we built a mouse (lemming) trap by setting a choice kernel beneath a heavy stone that rested on a plate held up by a piece of flint. The stone was meant to come crashing down upon the lemming-thief when the kernel was moved. When the mousetrap worked and the little lemming lay dead beneath the stone, I was heartbroken. So what is it? Is all life important? Where to draw the line? I want to be respectful, but even in the wanting to be, it isn't always easy to know what to do until the situation arises.

When the lemming's partner appeared a few days later, Tobias and I decided to let her take as many popcorn kernels as she wanted.

| 32 |

FIRST LIGHT

Our sleeping rhythm adjusted to whatever natural light we were exposed to. In the summer, when the sun almost never disappeared, bedtime was at two or three in the morning and we woke up at seven or eight, never feeling tired. If I had nights like that in Zurich, I'd be weary all day long. In Alaska there was never a problem with loss of energy. On the other hand, in Switzerland eight hours was a long night's sleep, but in Alaska during the wintertime ten hours of sleep was common.

By the middle of January, Tobias and I began to hope for and look for the sun. Going out on ski excursions in the Fall had allowed us to locate the highest mountain ridge to the east. We weren't sure exactly what day the sun would return, so we began hiking up our eastern mountain every day from the beginning of the third week in January, wanting to be right on the ridge when the first rays of the new-born orb filtered over the top.

We would rush up the mountain a little way, and climb upon a rock pile.

"Can you see it?" I'd call to Tobias because his pile was higher than mine.

"Nope," he'd answer.

Then we rushed up a little higher to climb onto another pile of rocks.

"Can you see it?" Tobias would shout to me.

"Not yet!" I'd answer. "But I know it's coming!"

We were like kids watching and waiting for Santa Claus. We climbed to the top of the ridge for a whole week until one day, after sixty-six days of darkness, the sun peeked over the horizon. We removed the woolen scarves that covered our faces and felt the warmth of the sun's fingers on our skin. Sixty-six days of darkness. Sixty-six days without the sun. Even though I knew, in the darkest winter during the longest storm, that the sun would come again, seeing it appear in the distance and feeling its semblance of warmth on that late day in January was like a miracle. Somehow it was like being born again.

During the first week of February a herd of caribou ambled into our valley. All of the animals sported great tufts of white fur at their chests, making them look as if they all had costumed beards. They used their hooves to dig away the hardened snow and grazed on lichen and moss that lay underneath. We watched them daily. They were beautiful, stately creatures that huddled together when the wind blew, and cavorted about when the air was quiet. After two weeks of consuming all the lichen our little valley had to offer, they were gone.

Later in the month, and from a distance, we became acquainted with a wolverine. A wolverine walks like a bear, but is much smaller, smaller than a husky, even, but much more dangerous. Bears and moose will run away from a wolverine. It has very sharp teeth, and is perhaps the most aggressive animal in the wild.

I had a book with track and scat drawings, so one day on a hike I saw some tracks that I presumed were from a wolverine. We were quite far from the cabin when we noticed a splash of dark moving some distance from us. Hoping it was a black bear rather than a wolverine, I took out my binoculars and watched as the spot crept closer. I couldn't smell the animal, which wasn't a good sign, because bears have quite a strong smell. They eat everything --- fruit, animals, even plastic to get to the food beneath --- and their bodies stink. Then I realized we were upwind from whatever creature it was who approached us, and it was probably smelling us. I looked through my binoculars again. It was a wolverine.

He crept below a large rock that was about four or five hundred feet away, then moved his head out to get a protected but clear view of us. We just stood there and watched him watching us. All of a sudden he darted out from behind the rock and headed straight toward us!

This could not be good.

And I figured that if a bear runs from a wolverine, and if a moose runs from a wolverine, it was probably wise that we run from the wolverine, too. We had no stick to defend ourselves with, although we did have our snowshoes strapped to our backpacks that we could use as weapons. But that was the problem. The snowshoes were strapped to our backpacks. We had no time to unstrap them.

We were near the top of a mountain, and because hard snow covered the mountain, it was easy to run across it. Running up one way and down the other as speedily as possible, we found camouflage behind a series of snowdrifts. The wolverine was left somewhere on the other side.

| 33 |

SIGNS & REALITY

We laughed at the craziness of it. Who knew we were so fast? We congratulated each other on not having been bitten by the wolverine's sharp teeth, and on having seen one of Alaska's rarest of creatures. After looking two or three more times behind our hardened snow drift to make sure the wolverine wasn't still on our tracks, we sighed with satisfaction, unstrapped our snow shoes, and skied home.

Home.

The little cabin in the frozen wasteland of the Ray Mountains had become our home. There was no plumbing, no electricity, and for cooking and washing we had to carry water from the stream outside. The whole hut was one room made of pine logs. On the wooden roof Robert Agen had placed grass sod, knowing that its roots would cling to the logs and keep them in place.

The hut had no fireplace, but it did have a stove and a brand new stovepipe. The stove was fixed in place between dark wood cabinets nailed to one wall. A long table ran the length of another wall under one of the hut's three windows. The cabin had platforms for our sleeping bags, two chairs, a grain grinder, a bucket, and our candles. The hut was simple. Barren. But it was all heaven to me and I loved it because it reminded me so much of the cabin my family had visited in the Alps before my father died.

What separated this cabin from that one, however, was the piece

of art painted into the panels of the interior side of the entrance door. While studying the painting for the first time, I was touched by it, almost as much as I was touched by the Northern Lights.

I was surprised by my joy upon seeing a work of art in the wilderness. It was an unanticipated, delicate painting created by a fellow human being. I had expected to be alone with my own thoughts and feelings out in the barren Ray Mountains, and here someone had left a message. I found spiritual significance in each of the image's parts because the artist's style was similar to mine. But in the end I concluded it wasn't necessary to determine the correct meaning of the artwork. It was enough to simply recognize the feelings that the painting evoked in me. The painting let me feel --- know, understand --- that I was meant to be in this place, and that I was not alone. I passed that painting every day, sometimes looking at it closely, other times ignoring it completely and concentrating only on the task that awaited inside or out. If a person doesn't want to see something, he can shut himself off from seeing it, even if all the people around him can see it very clearly. Sometimes it's hard to face reality, and for many years I had been in the habit of shutting reality out.

In Alaska I examined small moments --- small things that happened --- like meeting an Eskimo who lived with forgiveness in his heart, like a bear that walked away as I stood motionless nearby, like the Northern Lights, like choosing one way in November rather than another to walk back to Fairbanks, like surviving a fall into a frozen stream, like this painting --- collectively they were a book full of signs that I encountered --- because I was in Alaska --- that proved I was not alone. During the winter I became progressively aware of the fact that all of these things were actually *signs*, and then I began to understand that I needed to learn once again how to trust the Reality behind the signs.

I had blamed God for taking my father away when I needed him. And perhaps a hidden reason for coming to Alaska, home to more than half the glaciers in the world, was to be in contact with my emotionally cold father again.

Unexpectedly through Tobias, I was. It was Tobias who enabled me to see my father, because my father was still residing very comfortably inside of me. I hadn't realized this because I had

never before taken note of how many of my father's character traits I possessed. Tobias brought out the similarities when he unconsciously acted out the role of the child in our relationship, and I was forced to act out the role of the father.

It was Tobias' nightmare on the river-with-no-flood that awakened me to the realization of the similarities my father and I shared, and from then on I became acutely aware of every belittling word or critical look that escaped me. From then on I would take time to reflect on the harsh way I was treating Tobias, which I hated, just as I hated the aloof and frosty way my father had treated me. I hated being misunderstood, ignored, and belittled by my father. I hated that he didn't share the knowledge of his skill with me freely. I hated that he wouldn't speak to me. And I hated to see how much I was like him.

In my youth I had blamed God for taking my Vati away because I loved him, but in Alaska, after admitting the hate I felt for my father, I wanted to blame God for removing him from my life because I hadn't been given time to work out all these conflicting emotions.

Gradually, though, I was able to let go of the blame all together. If I could forgive God for taking my Vati, perhaps he could forgive me for thinking I was God --- that I had the power to control everything around me --- that I was invincible.

Certain words the Eskimo said struck me profoundly, and I carried them with me through the winter. These certain words implied that if I were willing to trust, then things would be as they should for me. Throughout the winter I resisted giving in to this philosophy completely... because I knew deep inside that I needed to conduct a different kind of *Weiterbildung* first...the kind which would allow me to gain more information about the Light of the World, and about the Being in whom I needed to trust.

Alaska transported me to my physical, mental, and emotional limits, and I was made to face the fact that no matter how much I had prepared, I could not save myself. I was not invincible. For certain, someone was watching over me. There was someone guiding me, leading me, and wanting to share secrets of the earth with me. On the darkest night, in the iciest river, through the

fiercest storm, there was someone who had allowed me to become warm again.

At twelve years old I had shut out protective warning pictures from my life, but after Alaska I was ready to welcome them back again.

| 34 |

READY OR NOT

"Good snow won't last past March," Harold had warned us. "But enough of it should still be on the ground toward the end of March to support a landing for my plane."

So Tobias and I agreed that with the assistance of Harold and his plane we would abandon our mountain retreat on the twenty-first of March.

Except Harold was wrong about the snow. All during the beginning of March wind was lifting most of the loose white powder on the flatland and depositing it over the rocks and fields and vales around the cabin.

The rough "runway" would need to be padded with snow somehow, so a week before we expected Harold, Tobias and I began carting sleds full of snow from the surrounding fields and dumping those piles along a ten-foot wide strip in the fattest part of the valley. We hoped to lengthen that strip to at least one hundred yards. Every day we added snow. The air temperature in March was about thirty-five degrees Fahrenheit during the day, but where the sun shone it was much warmer. So while snow was being added to a new part of the runway, existing snow on the older part melted away. There was serious concern whether Harold would really be able to land on such a bumpy piece of terrain.

Nevertheless, we packed our supplies, cleaned out the cabin, contributed two gallons of kerosene and our leftover food to

the cache, and made ourselves ready to leave immediately when Harold reached us.

On the morning of March twenty-first, we saw the plane before hearing it.

At that precise moment, the moment I saw Harold's plane, there was a *PANG* deep in the pit of my stomach, like the strike of a hammer. The airplane was a clear and unmistakable signal that our retreat into the wilderness had ended. "This is it," I said out loud to stifle any more panging.

Harold landed with a few bumps and lurches, but had no serious problem. I stood immobile as he came to a stop. *PANG*.

Would I ever be ready to leave? During the winter I had found the place for which I had searched most of my life. Time in the Ray Mountains --- time away from work and the stress of deadlines and city crowds --- had allowed me to experience an astonishing freedom. Freedom to think and schedule as I pleased meant never having to explain anything to anyone. Most importantly, the experience went as hoped: I learned that I was very comfortable being out in the wild. I became a part of it. I became confident that, even if unable to grow sprouts or any other type of fruit or vegetable, I could have survived, even thrived, off the land.

After the many lengthy internal debates regarding killing-a-moose versus killing-Ptarmigan versus killing-fish, I allowed the Athabascans and Eskimos to be my guides. Athabascans and Eskimos eat the flesh of animals for survival, and I eventually decided that if I absolutely had to trap birds for sustenance, I would have. If there were not plenty of birds to trap, and if birds wouldn't satisfy, I then would have trapped moose and elk and become a red-meat-eater. All Alaska Natives have great respect for the earth and all its creatures great and small, and on them they depend for their survival. So if needed, I would have, too.

My experience in Alaska was also more than I hoped. I came to know myself better. Through Tobias I came to see parts of me that I didn't like, and was thankful to witness change. I even came to the place where I could forgive my father, because I recognized how impossible it is for a person to change the parts of himself he doesn't like without seeing, without focusing honestly on his

actions and attitudes, and without reflecting on them. I forgive my father now, because I understand how difficult it is to change when you don't have someone help you see.

Tobias never blamed me for anything. He accepted whatever came his way. "Just say hello to the dentist for me," he had said while deep in the forest of a lost mountain days or perhaps weeks away from warmth and rest. With him I never had to explain myself. We both accepted whatever came our way, even all the storms. In a way, I was glad for so many of them. They minimized our plans and possibilities for exploring outside, and allowed for more internal exploration.

There was no wind on the twenty-first, and Harold needed wind to take off. How ironic. Maybe we'd have to wait a day or two, or maybe we'd have to prolong our stay for ten or twelve days more.

But the twenty-first was meant to be the day of departure.

"No problem leaving this morning," Harold assured us after he landed. He was flying a small, light supercub with little skis next to the wheels. It could hold four people. On one of the four seats we arranged some of our supplies, and the rest of the stuff we stacked in the back. I enjoyed one last look around the cabin, one last look at the stream, and one last look through the woods into the valley. Tobias was not with me as I said my goodbyes. Perhaps he had his own ritual.

When Harold saw us standing near the aircraft once more, he threw us his ropes. We ran alongside the supercub and when the plane was turned, jumped inside. The plane lifted effortlessly, and we were on our way. Outside my window the valley shrunk to the image of a black ribbon cutting a swath across a white and gray canvas. Well, it would no longer be my valley. I would not be back. I was leaving the Ray Mountains for good. *PANG.*

The panging drove me to consider other ways to remain in Alaska. Once back in Fairbanks I learned that a couple of Peter's friends had started a wilderness guide business and were seeking a guide who spoke English, German and French. As no American had applied for the position, I did so, got the job and was awarded a Green Card in the process. This Green Card assured permission to remain in the United States beyond the one-and-a-half-year

time-frame that my passport Immigration Stamp allowed. While deciding whether or not to accept this position, another possibility opened up. Would I like to work for a professor at the University of Alaska? The professor was friends with Peter and Fabienne and one day saw the log cabin that we had built. He asked if we could build him a much bigger one on the Tanana River. He promised to pay well for our work.

Two job offers meant options. Having options is always good.

The first job would require making it possible for ordinary people to trek into the wilderness and let them pretend to be adventurers. Questions resounded in my brain like popcorn. Why should I take people into the wilderness as if they were simply going into an amusement park? If they were not amusement park-type people, what kind of people would they be? Would they be tourists on a schedule, anxious to get back to their martinis and hot tubs when a storm came upon them? Would these tourists be open to watching, waiting, listening? Would they be willing to join the Wilderness? Would they let the Wilderness come into their beings? My whole organism resisted revealing secrets of the Wild to people who had done nothing to plan or prepare to survive in it. The closer the time came for me to make a decision the stronger the resistance. I concluded that I could not be involved with such a process. Working for the wilderness guide company simply wasn't in the cards.

I imagined the second job being a pleasurable and creative challenge. The process of helping Peter build his log cabin had been quite enjoyable. But the idea of having someone else tell me what to build and how to build it, set me on a schedule, put me back on a grid, made my stomach churn more than pang.

I became convinced that having to work in Alaska to earn money would change my experience of it completely.

I didn't want to change my experience, but work would be necessary to provide living expenses.

In the end I concluded that living in Alaska on a more permanent basis would be like living on an island. I would be isolated and protected from any issue I didn't want to address. Because of this, and in spite of the harsh conditions, living there seemed too easy

an approach to life.

And taking the easy way was not my style. I desired to continue to grow, which required confronting even unpleasant things, like resolving the relationship with my non-talking mother, reticent sister, the friends I had criticized, and the creative work inside me that still remained untapped. Resolving these issues couldn't be done in Alaska. I needed to return to Switzerland, sort out the new information learned in Alaska regarding who I am, and discover who I could become. That required returning to my place of birth. Was I ready and willing to face that challenge? If so, a kind of preparation and work I had always resisted in the past would be required.

35

GOING FORWARD

After stepping off the plane in Zurich, throngs of people surrounded me and speeding cars rushed at me like a winter storm in the Alaskan wilderness. They were noises and forces of movement that came at me as if I were in a dark tunnel. Except it was broad daylight.

My cousin Cedric invited me to live with him and his family. It was hard coming out of an environment of simplicity and silence and aloneness, then staying day after day in a small apartment with two other adults and two small children. But low on money, I had no other option. In Alaska I felt myself open, strong, healthy, filled, and happy. It was the best year of my life. In coming back to Switzerland, all that was left behind.

I fell into a deep depression. If I had gone to a psychiatrist, he would have prescribed medication, but I didn't want to approach a cure for depression with drugs.

Attempting to analyze myself and determine what was wrong resulted in physical illness --- tonsillitis, to be specific.

For the six months I lived with Cedric, I worked for a fledgling manufacturing company designing backpacks, and when I found a small house to rent, moved out and lived alone on the outskirts of Zurich. I ended up getting tonsillitis six different times in the next year.

After going to a hospital in Zurich, I was passed from physician to

physician. None wanted to remove the tonsils to provide me relief from throat-pain and fevers ("a short-term benefit," they called it), insisting that not having my tonsils in the long-term would be detrimental to my body's overall ability to fight disease. So they turned me into a laboratory specimen, and during one series of tests let it be known that they were coming to the conclusion that I was HIV positive. At that time AIDS was mostly a homosexual disease, and after being in the wilderness for one year with one other man, all of the doctors couldn't help but assume that I was a homosexual. I assured them I was not.

On the day they rendered their doctors' report, many painful tests were performed on me. I decided then that this would be the last visit to any physician for tonsillitis. Carrying a low-grade fever and chills, I left the doctors and their hospital saying, "You won't see me again."

Some friends that I skied with before Alaska referred me to a homeopathic doctor they thought I should talk to. And that's what the homeopathic doctor and I did. We just talked. He said, "We could do all those tests for your heart and kidneys and liver, but I'm sure there's no problem with your organs. I suggest that you face your sickness in another way."

This homeopath pushed the first domino, and I was ready to begin healing. He opened another path, away from my grid. I talked, and the doctor responded. There were two of us in his office: one person talking, the other one listening, and then responding. How different that was compared to what happened between Tobias and me. When Tobias and I found ourselves all alone in the cabin in winter, when we had nobody to talk to but each other, I wanted to have some response from him. I appreciated his trust, but preferred a response. I needed to hear what he thought.

In the middle of the winter I offered a prediction. "When we go back to Switzerland, we will split up. We will say good-bye, and probably never see each other again. We've gone through a lot of experiences together, but we're not getting to know each other. We haven't become friends. This kind of partnership won't last in Switzerland." At that moment I felt like shaking him and demanding that he tell me something. Anything. But even this sad

vision of the future changed neither Tobias' ability nor desire to communicate more. I always resorted to asking questions, because Tobias would never speak up himself. Sadly Tobias was just a shadow of his father.

It wasn't coincidental that we went to Alaska together. I wasn't in the habit of speaking a lot then, either. But I spoke volumes in comparison to him. And the silence in the cabin begged for him to express his deepest thoughts and feelings.

Tobias did work on himself, though. He went through mighty changes. Inside and out. Even the way he stood changed. When I first met Tobias, he had very little body strength. His muscles were soft and weak. In addition, Tobias could often make himself invisible. By this I mean that he was always withdrawing into the background of a group. He was there, but no one spoke to him. No one seemed to notice him. He took himself out of the happenings. Out of life. He often looked to the ground.

When we arrived back in Fairbanks after the winter away, Harold dropped us off at the airport, and there stood Tobias. You saw him as a fully-formed man. And he was talking with someone, another pilot who was asking him how the weather had been for the flight.

In Denali Park in April, Tobias and I tented and hiked around. One day Austrian mountaineers showed up. They had been climbing Mt. McKinley. Words spilled out of Tobias' mouth in his excitement to tell about our stay in the Ray Mountains. He talked as he had never talked before. The Austrians were impressed that we had stayed alone in some far away mountains all winter without a radio. They listened to Tobias with great admiration, and asked many questions which he answered without hesitation. As we walked away, Tobias' chest was expanded and his head was held high. "Did you hear what they said?" he asked. "Did you hear? They said they admired us, even though they were the ones who had climbed Mt. McKinley."

A few weeks after returning to Switzerland, I spoke with people from the canoe club in St. Gallen who reported their amazement at the great change that Tobias had gone through.

"He moved out of his parents' house and got an apartment right

away," one said.

"Who is this person who's talking all the time now? Is it really the same Tobias?" another asked.

"He's become quite opinionated!" someone else joked.

Later I heard that Tobias had participated in some vigorous mountain climbing expeditions. He even traveled as far as Asia to scale Mt. Everest, the tallest mountain in the world. Tobias did phone me once to tell me he had decided to study Information Technology. The second call was to tell me that he had gotten a job as a computer specialist.

Each of these reports encouraged me.

Before Alaska, Tobias was tied to all of the connections and habits of St. Gallen. Afterwards, he was free. He had died to the old person. He wasn't the "same" Tobias. He was new. In Alaska I often thought that the Tobias of St. Gallen had been manipulated by his parents as if he were a radio-controlled toy. Up until the time he left for Alaska, he was a little boy, afraid of making mistakes. He was afraid of answering questions anyone posed to him.

But in Alaska that little boy died, and he became a man.

ABOUT THE AUTHOR

Not until many years after leaving the Allgemeine Gewerbeschule (now called the Basel School of Design) in Basel, Switzerland, was I able to fully realize what a unique place it had been.

The school officially opened in 1968, but Swiss design master Armin Hofmann, along with typography guru Emil Ruder, had been training small groups of students for a number of years before that. They had gathered together a group of like-minded teachers in Basel in order to advance an understanding of sound graphic design principles to art students from around the world.

Because I became a student at the Allgemeine Gewerbeschule in Basel I am now a part of the Emil Ruder – Armin Hofmann – Wolfgang Weingart – Kurt Hauert – Peter von Arx history of Graphic Design.

I am also a part of Ruedi Glauser's history, because it was in Basel, at the Allgemeine Gewerbeschule, that I met the subject of this book.

Ruedi's desk sat catty-corner to mine, so whenever I had a question about an assignment, was confused by a Swiss-German word, or needed to have a Swiss tradition explained, I could whisper my question to Ruedi and he was happy to help clarify.

Ruedi also shared his mountains with me. The Alps --- his Alps --- were where physical and emotional senses I hadn't even known I possessed awakened. Taking trips into the mountains and learning about the traditions that enliven them caused me to develop a profound respect for a country that came to feel more and more like home. And my friendship with Ruedi challenged me to think more like an artist by refusing to be satisfied with doing the minimum for any piece of work. He challenged me to *go further...*

When Ruedi told me of his plan to go to Alaska, I was one of those who thought he was crazy.

How could anyone live on the frozen tundra...in a tent...for weeks, or even months, on end? How could anyone stay warm? What would he eat? Where would he brush his teeth or wash his hair? Could anyone survive that? And was he really going alone?

I had to know his story. And over the course of a year, he told it to me, bit by bit. Bear by bear. Bird by bird.

His story opened my eyes and challenged me. After hearing it, I knew it needed a much wider audience.

Currently I have one daughter and live with my husband in South Florida, where I practice graphic design, acting in TV and print commercials, and helping others tell their stories in writing. I also continue to miss the mountains.

To find out more about this and other books by the author,
or if you'd like help telling your story,
visit:
www.kriswilliamsauthor.com

Printed in Great Britain
by Amazon

74231446R00147